Elevate Your Enterprise

Mastering the Art of Small Business Expansion

THOMAS DEVANE

Table of content

Introduction

In the dynamic theater of commerce, where small businesses stand as both the heartbeat of innovation and the embodiment of entrepreneurial dreams, a select few emerge not only as survivors but as victors. They transcend the ordinary, growing beyond the constraints of their modest origins to commandeer vast landscapes of success. This book, "Elevate Your Enterprise: Mastering the Art of Small Business Expansion," is a meticulous blueprint for those who seek not merely to grow, but to ascend the summit of their potential.

Consider the story of Renaissance Interiors, a tale echoing in the chambers of business lore. What once was a modest interior design studio flourished into an empire of aesthetic sophistication, captivating discerning clientele and inspiring a wave of aspirants. The journey of Renaissance Interiors mirrors the very essence of the narrative etched within these pages – the transformation of humble origins into extraordinary stature.

Imagine, for a moment, walking into the early days of Renaissance Interiors. Sarah, the visionary founder, meticulously sketching designs on a worn drafting table, fueled by an unwavering dedication to elegance. With each project she undertook, a symphony of creativity emerged, intertwining client visions with artistic ingenuity. As word of her distinct touch spread, a faithful following emerged, eager to experience the alchemy of her designs.

The journey, however, was far from seamless. New challengers, rising with the dawn of trends, threatened to eclipse Renaissance Interiors' brilliance. Yet, adversity summoned innovation. Sarah's evolution from craftsman to strategist was a pivot that anchored her position and expanded her influence. The studio's collaboration with virtual reality technology was not merely a technological stride; it was a calculated leap into the future, bridging the tangible and the digital.

"Elevate Your Enterprise" stands as a tribute to the tales of fortitude like Renaissance Interiors. It embraces the nuances that demand mastery: understanding the symphony of market dynamics, orchestrating operations for harmonious efficiency, and composing the grand overture of brand expansion. This volume is not a mere guide; it is a testament to the philosophy that the road to triumph in business is illuminated by strategy, informed by wisdom, and enriched by relentless aspiration.

In the chapters that follow, you will traverse the intricate landscape of growth – from redefining your business identity and crafting an irresistible brand, to forging marketing campaigns that resonate in the digital age. You will decipher the labyrinth of finance, dissecting budgets, investments, and funding streams with surgical precision.

Moreover, you will explore the symposium of people, decoding the art of team composition, leadership refinement, and the orchestration of collective genius.

Let the pages of this volume be your compass, guiding you through the realm where intention becomes strategy, and strategy births growth. Whether you're a tyro entrepreneur grasping for the first rung of the ladder or a seasoned architect of enterprises seeking to add new dimensions, the principles encapsulated herein transcend experience, time, and industry.

Embrace these words not merely as insights, but as a compass that steers you towards the fulcrum of growth, excellence, and mastery. "Elevate Your Enterprise" is your artifact of transformation, your invitation to join the ranks of visionaries who dared to dream big and dared to ascend even higher. Let the journey commence.

Understanding the Importance of Business Growth

In the symphony of business, growth isn't just a catchy tune; it's the resonating chord that defines the very rhythm of success. As the curtains rise on the grand theater of commerce, the spotlight falls on a central truth: stagnation is the antithesis of evolution. In this chapter, we delve into the profound significance of business growth, unveiling the rationale that propels the most triumphant enterprises towards perpetual advancement.

The Anatomy of Business Growth

Imagine a sapling on fertile ground. It begins as a fragile shoot, nurtured by sunlight, water, and time. As it stretches its tendrils towards the heavens, it evolves into a sturdy tree, its branches embracing the sky with unwavering resilience. In similar fashion, a business starts with an idea, cultivated with dedication and determination. It germinates, transforming into an entity that not only sustains its creators but also enriches the lives of its stakeholders.

A Competitive Landscape

In the digital age, where innovation reigns supreme, standing still is tantamount to relinquishing your place in the market. The tapestry of commerce is woven with a multitude of businesses vying for attention, striving to differentiate themselves from the rest. Growth isn't just a choice; it's a strategic imperative. The evolution from a fledgling enterprise to an industry leader is the ultimate testament to a business's resilience and adaptability.

Economies of Scale and Opportunities

Consider the power of economies of scale – the concept where unit costs decrease as production quantities increase. Growth provides businesses the leverage to negotiate better deals with suppliers, reduce production costs, and optimize processes. Moreover, expansion into new markets opens the gateway to previously untapped opportunities. As your business grows, so does your ability to explore uncharted territories, conquer new customer segments, and diversify revenue streams.

Attracting Talents and Resources

Success begets success. A growing business, one that resonates with a vision of a brighter future, draws not only customers but also talented individuals seeking to contribute to that vision. The allure of being part of a thriving, expanding entity is magnetic. Moreover, growth provides access to greater financial resources, allowing for investments in innovation, research, and development that bolster the core competency of your enterprise.

Cultivating Resilience and Innovation

The trajectory of growth is seldom a straight line; it's a tapestry woven with challenges and triumphs. Navigating these challenges instills resilience, shaping your business to withstand market fluctuations and unforeseen disruptions. Moreover, growth necessitates constant innovation, as you must evolve to meet the changing needs and preferences of your expanding customer base.

In the grand mosaic of business, growth is the brushstroke that paints the canvas with hues of prosperity and promise. Beyond being a financial metric, growth is a philosophy – a mindset that transcends complacency, embraces change, and charts a course towards excellence. As you proceed through the chapters of this book, remember: understanding the importance of business growth is not merely a revelation; it's a compass guiding you towards a brighter, bolder tomorrow.

Setting the Stage for Growth

Like a director preparing a stage for an epic performance, a business must meticulously set the scene before the crescendo of growth begins. In this chapter, we embark on a strategic journey that lays the foundation for sustainable and purposeful expansion. Just as an architect envisions the blueprint before construction commences, so too must an entrepreneur craft a roadmap for growth that is both visionary and pragmatic.

Cultivating the Growth Mindset

The genesis of growth is the mindset that dares to envision beyond the status quo. It's about shedding the comfort of familiarity and embracing the possibilities that lie in uncharted territory. A growth mindset thrives on curiosity, innovation, and a relentless pursuit of excellence. It's about nurturing a culture where every team member sees challenges as opportunities and change as an inherent part of progress.

Strategic Planning: Your Blueprint for Success

Setting the stage requires meticulous planning. A well-crafted strategic plan becomes your compass, guiding you through the labyrinth of decisions and actions. It involves analyzing your current position, envisioning your future, and charting the course to bridge the gap. Your strategic plan is not a static document; it's a living entity that evolves with your business, adapting to shifting landscapes and unforeseen opportunities.

Defining Clear Objectives and Key Results (OKRs)

Objectives and Key Results (OKRs) are the constellations that guide your strategic voyage. Objectives define the destination you seek – the audacious goals that stretch your business's capabilities. Key Results are the measurable milestones that indicate your progress toward those objectives. This framework aligns your entire organization toward a common purpose and creates a culture of accountability.

Risk Assessment and Mitigation

In the theater of business, growth isn't without its share of risks. Just as a ship prepares for rough waters, a business must assess potential pitfalls and strategize for their mitigation. Conduct a comprehensive risk assessment, identifying both internal and external factors that could impede your progress. Develop contingency plans that safeguard your journey and empower you to navigate uncertainties with resilience.

Resource Allocation and Scalable Infrastructure

Growth demands resources – financial, human, and technological. Assess your resource allocation strategy to ensure it aligns with your expansion goals. From a sturdy technological infrastructure that can accommodate increased demand to a recruitment strategy that secures the talent needed for growth, every resource must be optimized for scalability.

Cultivating Partnerships and Alliances

Just as a play thrives on the synergy of its cast, a business thrives on strategic partnerships and alliances. Collaborations with complementary businesses can unlock new markets, enhance product offerings, and amplify brand reach. Building a network of like-minded partners is akin to assembling an ensemble that enhances the collective performance.

Setting the stage for growth isn't a singular event; it's a continuous process of preparation, adaptation, and execution. It's about creating an environment where growth is not an accident, but a result of purposeful actions and aligned strategies. As you delve into the pages that follow, remember that setting the stage is more than just a prelude; it's a commitment to crafting a narrative of enduring success, where growth is not just a destination, but a transformative journey.

Defining Your Growth Strategy

In the realm of business, growth is not an abstract concept; it's a well-crafted strategy that paves the way for expansion, innovation, and impact. This chapter delves into the pivotal process of defining your growth strategy – a compass that guides your business toward its desired future. Just as a composer arranges notes to create a symphony, so too must an entrepreneur orchestrate a growth strategy that harmonizes vision with action.

Evaluating Your Current Position

Before embarking on any journey, understanding your starting point is crucial. Assess the current state of your business –

its strengths, weaknesses, opportunities, and threats. This introspection provides the canvas upon which your growth strategy is painted. By analyzing financial health, market position, and operational efficiency, you gain the clarity needed to navigate the path ahead.

Identifying Growth Opportunities

Growth is not a one-size-fits-all endeavor. It's about capitalizing on opportunities that align with your business's unique strengths and market trends. Explore avenues such as market penetration, product development, diversification, and geographic expansion. Your growth strategy should be a mosaic of carefully selected opportunities that resonate with your long-term vision.

Choosing the Right Growth Path: Organic vs. Inorganic

The growth path you choose shapes the trajectory of your business's evolution. Organic growth involves expanding your current operations through increased sales, new product lines, or enhanced marketing efforts. Inorganic growth, on the other hand, involves mergers, acquisitions, and partnerships. Each path carries its own set of benefits and challenges; your choice should align with your resources, objectives, and risk tolerance.

Crafting a Vision for Growth

A well-defined growth strategy is more than a tactical plan; it's a narrative that encapsulates your business's aspirations.

Craft a clear and compelling vision that paints a vivid picture of what success looks like in the future. This vision not only galvanizes your team but also serves as a North Star that guides decision-making, fosters alignment, and instills a sense of purpose.

Allocating Resources Strategically

Your growth strategy should not be an abstraction; it should be a roadmap for resource allocation. Determine the financial, human, and technological resources required to execute your strategy. Allocate these resources with precision, ensuring that they align with your growth priorities and contribute to achieving your defined objectives.

Measuring Progress and Iterating

Growth is not a linear journey; it's a continuous cycle of assessment, action, and adjustment. Define key performance indicators (KPIs) that quantify the success of your growth strategy. Regularly monitor these metrics, evaluate progress, and be prepared to pivot if the data indicates the need for course correction. Iteration is not a sign of failure but a hallmark of adaptability.

Defining your growth strategy is akin to sketching the blueprint of a grand architectural marvel. It's about aligning aspirations with actions, crafting a roadmap that transforms dreams into reality. As you delve deeper into this chapter, remember that your growth strategy isn't a static document; it's a living guide that evolves as your business does. Your strategy becomes the symphony conductor, guiding the various elements of your business toward harmonious growth and meaningful impact.

Assessing Your Current Business Position

In the realm of business, clarity is power. Before setting sail on the waters of growth, it's imperative to take stock of where you stand – to understand the landscape, strengths, weaknesses, and opportunities that shape your journey. This chapter is your compass for navigating the process of assessing your current business position, a critical step that illuminates the path to sustainable growth.

The Strategic Imperative of Assessment

Imagine a seasoned explorer embarking on a new quest. Before plotting the course, they meticulously study maps, climate patterns, and terrains. Similarly, assessing your business's current position provides the foundation for informed decision-making. This scrutiny unveils insights that shape your growth strategy and minimizes the pitfalls of unforeseen challenges.

Financial Health and Performance Metrics

The financial landscape of your business is the bedrock upon which growth is built. Scrutinize financial statements, cash flow patterns, and profitability ratios. Understand revenue trends, cost structures, and debt obligations. By quantifying your financial health, you pinpoint areas that require improvement and identify opportunities for investment.

Market Position and Competitive Landscape

The marketplace is a dynamic ecosystem where your business interacts with competitors, customers, and trends. Conduct a comprehensive analysis of your market position, evaluating your market share, customer segmentation, and competitive advantage. Understand your customers' needs, preferences, and pain points to tailor your growth strategy to their demands.

SWOT Analysis: Strengths, Weaknesses, Opportunities, and Threats

A SWOT analysis is your magnifying glass for assessing your business's internal and external factors. Identify your strengths –

the attributes that give you a competitive edge. Recognize weaknesses – areas that demand attention and improvement. Uncover opportunities – avenues for growth and innovation. Mitigate threats – potential challenges that could hinder your progress.

Operational Efficiency and Business Processes

Efficiency is the lifeblood of growth. Scrutinize your business's operational processes, identifying bottlenecks, redundancies, and areas of inefficiency. Streamline workflows, optimize supply chains, and embrace technological solutions that enhance productivity. A lean and agile operation is essential for scaling without compromising quality.

Customer Insights and Feedback

Your customers are more than mere transactions; they are your guiding compass. Solicit customer feedback, understand their satisfaction levels, and gather insights into their evolving needs. This data is invaluable for tailoring your growth strategy to meet customer expectations and enhance their overall experience.

Assessing your current business position isn't a mere formality; it's the cornerstone of strategic decision-making. It's about equipping yourself with an intimate understanding of your business's nuances, potentials, and vulnerabilities. As you navigate the intricacies of this chapter, remember that a clear assessment is the compass that directs your growth journey. It empowers you to make informed choices, capitalize on strengths, and navigate challenges with foresight. In the dynamic theater of business, understanding where you stand is the prelude to orchestrating your ascent.

Identifying Growth Opportunities

In the landscape of business, growth is more than a destination; it's a journey fueled by strategic choices and calculated risks. This chapter ventures into the realm of opportunity, where entrepreneurs become navigators of potential, charting courses that lead to expansion, innovation, and impact. Here, we explore the art and science of identifying growth opportunities that align with your vision and propel your business toward its full potential.

Navigating the Sea of Possibilities

Imagine your business as a vessel sailing on the vast sea of opportunities. Each opportunity is a distinct island waiting to be explored. By setting your sights on the horizon, you can discover new territories that hold the promise of growth. The art lies in identifying the opportunities that align with your business's unique strengths and market trends.

Market Penetration: Maximizing Existing Markets

Market penetration involves deepening your presence within your current market segments. This can be achieved by expanding your customer base, increasing the frequency of transactions, or gaining a larger share of customer spending. By leveraging your existing strengths and relationships, you can carve a deeper niche and strengthen your competitive position.

Product Development and Innovation

Innovation is the heartbeat of growth. Evaluate your existing products or services and seek opportunities for enhancement or diversification. Analyze customer feedback, industry trends, and technological advancements to identify areas where innovation can create value. By staying attuned to evolving customer needs, you can design solutions that resonate with your target audience.

Market Expansion: Exploring New Horizons

Venturing into new markets can open doors to untapped opportunities. Assess the feasibility of expanding geographically or targeting new customer segments. Research the cultural, economic, and regulatory nuances of these markets to tailor your offerings effectively. Expansion requires a keen understanding of the local landscape and a strategy that aligns with your global ambitions.

Diversification: Expanding Your Portfolio

Diversification involves entering new industries or adding complementary products/services to your existing lineup. While it offers the potential for growth, it also carries additional risk. Carefully evaluate the synergy between your current offerings and the new ventures to ensure they align with your core competencies and enhance your competitive advantage.

Strategic Partnerships and Collaborations

Collaboration can be a catalyst for growth. Identify opportunities to partner with other businesses that share a common target audience or complementary offerings. These partnerships can extend your reach, amplify your resources, and foster innovation through shared expertise. Choose partners whose values and goals align with your own to ensure a harmonious collaboration.

Digital Transformation and Technological Opportunities

In the digital era, technological advancements can be a springboard for growth. Assess opportunities to leverage technology to enhance customer experience, streamline operations, and open new avenues for revenue generation. Embrace digital tools, e-commerce platforms, data analytics, and automation to unlock efficiencies and connect with a broader audience.

Identifying growth opportunities is an art that requires a blend of creativity and strategic acumen. As you immerse yourself in this chapter, remember that each opportunity is a potential catalyst for your business's evolution. Your ability to discern and pursue the right opportunities is what sets you on the trajectory toward sustained growth. Just as an explorer seeks undiscovered lands, so too must you embark on this journey of opportunity, where the uncharted holds the promise of transformation.

Choosing the Right Growth Path: Organic vs. Inorganic Growth

In the realm of business expansion, the path you choose can significantly impact the trajectory of your growth journey. This chapter delves into the dichotomy of organic and inorganic growth, offering insights into the decision-making process that determines the most fitting avenue for your business. Just as a sculptor selects the right chisel for their masterpiece, so too must you choose the growth path that aligns with your vision, resources, and strategic goals.

Organic Growth: Nurturing from Within

Organic growth mirrors the natural process of nurturing and cultivating. It involves expanding your business using internal resources, gradually building upon your current foundation. This path is characterized by the slow and steady progression of market share, customer base, and revenue. Organic growth is a testament to the value you bring to your existing offerings and markets.

Advantages of Organic Growth

- Sustainable: Organic growth is often more sustainable over the long term. It's built on a solid foundation, minimizing the risk of overextending or compromising quality.

- Control: Since organic growth relies on internal resources, you have greater control over the pace and direction of expansion.

- Customer Loyalty: Organic growth is a testament to your ability to retain and satisfy existing customers, fostering strong relationships.

Inorganic Growth: Accelerating Expansion through External Means

Inorganic growth, on the other hand, involves expanding your business through external means, such as mergers, acquisitions, partnerships, or joint ventures. This path accelerates your growth trajectory by leveraging the strengths and resources of other entities. Inorganic growth can enable rapid market entry, enhanced capabilities, and access to new markets.

Advantages of Inorganic Growth

- Rapid Expansion: Inorganic growth can lead to rapid market entry and scaling, allowing you to capture new opportunities quickly.
- Access to Resources: Mergers or acquisitions can provide access to resources, technology, talent, and distribution networks that you might not have internally.
- Diversification: Inorganic growth allows for diversification beyond your current offerings or markets, reducing the risk associated with a single focus.
- Choosing Your Growth Path: Considerations and Criteria

The decision to pursue organic or inorganic growth is not one-size-fits-all; it depends on your business's unique circumstances, goals, and risk appetite. Consider the following factors when making your choice:

- Current Position: Evaluate your financial health, market presence, and operational capacity. Organic growth may be more suitable if you have a strong foundation and resources for gradual expansion.
- Speed: If you need rapid expansion, inorganic growth can expedite your entry into new markets or industries.
- Resources: Assess your financial resources, available talent, and technological capabilities. Inorganic

growth may require significant upfront investments.

- Risk Tolerance: Inorganic growth carries risks associated with integration, cultural alignment, and unforeseen challenges. Organic growth may be more controlled and less disruptive.

The choice between organic and inorganic growth is a pivotal one that shapes your business's trajectory. As you navigate this chapter, remember that your decision should be aligned with your vision, objectives, and available resources. Your growth path becomes a reflection of your strategic prowess — a testament to your ability to adapt, innovate, and execute. Just as an artist selects the right palette for their masterpiece, so too must you select the path that best resonates with your business's essence and aspirations.

Market Research and Analysis

In the dynamic realm of business, knowledge is not just power; it's the cornerstone of strategic decision-making. Market research and analysis illuminate the path to growth by providing insights into customer behavior, industry trends, and competitive dynamics. This chapter delves into the art and science of market research, equipping you with the tools to navigate the ever-changing landscape and position your business for success.

Understanding Your Target Audience

Imagine your business as a storyteller seeking to captivate an audience. Your target audience is the protagonist of this narrative – the individuals who engage with your products or services. Conduct thorough research to define your audience's demographics, preferences, pain points, and aspirations. This understanding allows you to tailor your offerings and messaging to resonate deeply.

Analyzing Market Trends and Dynamics

In the market's symphony, trends are the melodies that guide your composition. Analyze current and emerging trends that influence your industry – from technological advancements to shifting consumer preferences. Monitor changes in buying patterns, demand for specific features, and the adoption of new products or services.

This analysis arms you with the foresight needed to stay ahead of the curve.

Competitive Landscape and Benchmarking

In the arena of business, competitors are not adversaries; they are mirrors that reflect your own strengths and weaknesses. Conduct competitive analysis to understand your rivals' offerings, positioning, and strategies. Identify gaps in the market that you can fill or areas where you can differentiate. Benchmarking against industry leaders offers insights into best practices and areas for improvement.

SWOT Analysis Revisited

Just as a diamond reveals its facets under different angles of light, your business reveals nuances under the scrutiny of SWOT analysis. Revisit your strengths, weaknesses, opportunities, and threats in light of your market research findings. This synthesis provides a comprehensive understanding of how external factors intersect with your internal dynamics, guiding your growth strategy.

Customer Insights and Feedback

Your customers are more than statistics; they are the lifeblood of your business. Leverage customer feedback, reviews, and surveys to gain insights into their experiences. Understand their pain points, challenges, and the value they derive from your offerings. This qualitative data helps you refine your products, enhance your customer experience, and shape your growth trajectory.

Predictive Analysis and Data-driven Decisions

In the age of data, insights are gleaned not from intuition alone, but from data-driven analysis. Utilize predictive analysis to forecast market trends, demand patterns, and customer behavior. This empowers you to make informed decisions and allocate resources strategically, maximizing the impact of your growth initiatives.

Market research and analysis are not static exercises; they are continuous endeavors that inform your every move. As you immerse yourself in this chapter, remember that knowledge is your compass, and data is your guiding star. In the orchestra of business, market research sets the tempo, analysis orchestrates the harmony, and insights create the symphony that resonates with your target audience. Your mastery of market dynamics transforms uncertainty into strategy and possibilities into tangible growth.

Understanding Your Target Audience

In the intricate tapestry of business, your target audience is more than a demographic; they are the heartbeat that propels your success. This chapter delves into the art of understanding your target audience – a profound exploration that transcends mere data points and embraces the psychology, aspirations, and desires that guide consumer behavior. Just as a painter captures the essence of a subject's soul, so too must you immerse yourself in the essence of your audience to forge a connection that resonates.

Segmentation: Unveiling the Diversity Within

Your target audience is not a monolith; it's a mosaic of diverse individuals with unique needs and preferences. Segment your audience based on demographics, psychographics, and behavioral traits. This segmentation unveils nuances that empower you to tailor your marketing strategies, products, and messaging to different audience segments.

Creating Personas: Breathing Life into Data

Personas are the avatars that embody your audience segments. They are not fictional characters; they are distilled representations of your customers' personalities, values, and goals. Craft personas that go beyond surface-level data, delving into motivations, pain points, and the emotional journey that influences purchasing decisions.

Empathy Mapping: Stepping into Their Shoes

Empathy is the bridge that connects your business to your audience's hearts. Empathy mapping involves stepping into your audience's shoes and mapping their thoughts, feelings, and actions at every stage of their interaction with your brand. This deep understanding reveals opportunities to enhance customer experience and address pain points with precision.

Journey Mapping: Tracing the Path of Engagement

Imagine your audience's interaction with your brand as a journey – a series of touchpoints that shape their perception and loyalty. Journey mapping entails tracing this path, from awareness to post-purchase engagement. It reveals the highs and lows, the moments of delight and frustration, and offers insights into optimizing each interaction for maximum impact.

Analyzing Consumer Behavior: Unveiling the Why

Consumer behavior is not merely a sequence of actions; it's a canvas that paints the motivations behind those actions. Utilize data and research to decipher the psychological triggers that drive purchasing decisions. Understand the cognitive biases, emotional needs, and social influences that shape the way your audience engages with your offerings.

Feedback Loops and Continuous Learning

The relationship with your audience is an ongoing conversation, not a monologue. Create feedback loops that encourage customers to share their experiences, opinions, and suggestions. Analyze this feedback to refine your products, tailor your strategies, and demonstrate that you value their input.

Understanding your target audience is a journey that transcends statistics and embraces the essence of human connection.

As you immerse yourself in this chapter, remember that your audience is not a distant entity; they are individuals with dreams, aspirations, and challenges. Your ability to understand and empathize with them transforms marketing from transactional to transformative. Just as an author crafts characters with depth, so too must you unravel the complexities of your audience to create a narrative of resonance, trust, and lasting loyalty.

Analyzing Market Trends and Competition

In the ever-evolving landscape of business, success hinges on your ability to decipher the whispers of change and anticipate the rhythm of the market. This chapter delves into the dynamic realm of market trends and competition analysis – a strategic exploration that unveils the currents shaping your industry and the strategies of your rivals. Just as a navigator reads the stars to chart their course, so too must you read the signs to steer your business toward growth.

Unearthing Market Trends

Market trends are the footprints left by consumer behavior, technological advancements, and societal shifts. Harness the power of data and research to identify these trends. Study purchasing patterns, adoption rates of emerging technologies, and changes in customer preferences. Recognize the trends that are shaping your industry, and envision how they will influence your business in the future.

Spotting Disruptions and Innovations

Disruption is the symphony of change that reverberates across industries. Analyze the emergence of new technologies, business models, and market entrants that have the potential to reshape your landscape. Embrace innovation not only as a survival strategy but as a means to redefine your competitive edge and capitalize on the shifting tides of demand.

Staying Ahead of Consumer Behavior

Consumer behavior is a reflection of societal evolution. Study the cultural, economic, and psychological factors that influence how your audience interacts with your products or services. Analyze shifts in purchasing preferences, the growing significance of sustainability, and the impact of digital engagement on decision-making. Align your strategies with the evolving expectations of your customers.

Competitive Intelligence: The Art of Strategy

Your competitors are not adversaries; they are chess pieces on the board of strategy. Conduct competitive analysis to understand their strengths, weaknesses, positioning, and marketing strategies. Identify gaps in the market that your rivals have left unaddressed. This knowledge equips you to differentiate your offerings and seize opportunities that resonate with your audience.

Benchmarking Best Practices

In the symphony of business, the leaders are not just conductors; they are composers of best practices. Benchmark against industry leaders and innovators to gain insights into strategies that have propelled them to success. Adapt these practices to fit your business's unique context, enhancing your operational efficiency and customer engagement.

Staying Nimble and Adaptable

Market trends are not stationary; they are currents that shift with time. Your ability to stay nimble and adaptable is your secret weapon. Create processes for continuous monitoring of trends and competition. Be prepared to pivot your strategies in response to shifts in customer preferences, emerging technologies, or disruptive forces.

Analyzing market trends and competition is not a one-time endeavor; it's an ongoing process that fuels your business's agility and resilience. As you delve into this chapter, remember that trends are the guideposts that illuminate your path, and competition is the dynamic force that sharpens your strategic edge. Your mastery of this dance between insight and action empowers you to not only navigate change but to shape it. Just as a conductor harmonizes instruments to create a symphony, so too must you harmonize insights and strategies to orchestrate a narrative of sustainable growth and industry leadership.

Conducting SWOT Analysis

In the realm of business strategy, SWOT analysis stands as a powerful tool that unveils the landscape within which your enterprise operates. This chapter delves into the art of conducting a SWOT analysis – a comprehensive exploration of your business's strengths, weaknesses, opportunities, and threats. Just as an explorer maps uncharted territories, so too must you map the terrain of your business to chart a course toward growth and success.

Unveiling Your Strengths

Strengths are the pillars of your business – the attributes that set you apart and fuel your competitive advantage. Evaluate your internal resources, expertise, brand recognition, and unique selling propositions. Recognize the facets that make your business resilient, innovative, and trusted in the eyes of your customers.

Addressing Your Weaknesses

Weaknesses are the chinks in your armor – the areas that need attention and improvement. Candidly assess aspects of your business that are hindering growth or compromising efficiency. Identify operational bottlenecks, skill gaps, or deficiencies in customer experience. Addressing weaknesses empowers you to fortify your foundation and build a more robust business.

Seizing Opportunities

Opportunities are the open doors that invite growth and expansion. Analyze market trends, emerging technologies, and shifts in customer behavior to identify avenues where your business can thrive. Consider how you can leverage your strengths to capitalize on these opportunities and enhance your market presence.

Mitigating Threats

Threats are the storm clouds on the horizon – external factors that can disrupt your journey. Assess the competitive landscape, regulatory changes, economic shifts, and other external challenges that could impact your business. By recognizing threats early, you can develop strategies to mitigate their impact and enhance your resilience.

Creating Synergy: Matching Strengths and Opportunities

The synergy between strengths and opportunities is where growth flourishes. Identify areas where your strengths align with emerging opportunities. These intersections become the breeding grounds for innovation, new product development, and market expansion. Capitalize on these sweet spots to create maximum impact.

Transformation through Weaknesses and Threats

Weaknesses and threats are not roadblocks; they are catalysts for transformation. Develop strategies to address weaknesses and convert them into strengths. Similarly, create contingency plans to mitigate threats, minimizing their potential impact. These actions demonstrate adaptability and showcase your ability to navigate challenges.

Conducting a SWOT analysis is not a mere exercise; it's a strategic expedition that transforms insight into action. As you delve into this chapter, remember that SWOT analysis is not static; it's a dynamic tool that evolves with your business and the external environment. Your mastery of this process empowers you to navigate with clarity, capitalize on opportunities, and navigate challenges with foresight. Just as a cartographer maps uncharted lands, so too must you map the contours of your business to create a strategy that navigates with precision and purpose.

Building a Strong Brand Identity

In the vast landscape of business, a strong brand identity is the lighthouse that guides customers toward your shores. This chapter delves into the art of building a brand identity – a cohesive and compelling narrative that resonates with your audience, fosters trust, and sets your business apart. Just as an artist crafts a masterpiece, so too must you craft a brand identity that leaves an indelible mark on the canvas of your industry.

Defining Your Brand Essence

Your brand is more than a logo or a tagline; it's the essence that encapsulates your values, purpose, and promise. Define your brand's mission, vision, and core values. These elements form the foundation of your identity, guiding your decisions, actions, and interactions with customers.

Crafting Your Visual Identity

Visual identity is the face your brand presents to the world. Design a logo, select a color palette, and choose fonts that align with your brand's personality. These visual elements evoke emotions and become a recognizable symbol of your business. Consistency across all touchpoints reinforces your brand's authenticity and professionalism.

Telling Your Brand Story

A brand story is the thread that weaves your history, values, and offerings into a compelling narrative. Narrate your journey, the challenges you've overcome, and the impact you aim to make. A well-told story not only engages your audience but also humanizes your business, fostering a deeper connection.

Crafting a Unique Value Proposition

A unique value proposition (UVP) is the beacon that distinguishes your brand from the competition. Identify the unique benefits you offer to customers and articulate them in a clear and concise manner. Your UVP becomes the rallying cry that resonates with your target audience, addressing their pain points and showcasing your solutions.

Consistency across Touchpoints

A strong brand identity is a symphony that plays consistently across every touchpoint. Whether it's your website, social media, packaging, or customer service, ensure that your brand's messaging, tone, and visual elements remain cohesive. Consistency fosters trust and reinforces the image you want to portray.

Emotional Connection and Brand Loyalty

Brand loyalty is not merely a transactional bond; it's an emotional connection. Craft experiences that resonate with your audience on a personal level. Engage in meaningful interactions, listen to customer feedback, and create a sense of community around your brand. This emotional connection fosters customer loyalty that transcends price points.

Innovation and Evolution of Your Brand

A strong brand identity is not static; it evolves with your business and the changing market dynamics. Embrace innovation while staying true to your core values. As you expand your offerings or enter new markets, ensure that your brand's essence remains intact, even as its expression evolves.

Building a strong brand identity is not an exercise in aesthetics; it's a strategic endeavor that infuses your business with purpose and resonance. As you delve into this chapter, remember that your brand identity is not a façade; it's a reflection of your business's soul. Your mastery of this art empowers you to shape perceptions, foster loyalty, and stand as a beacon of authenticity in a sea of choices. Just as an architect designs with vision, so too must you design a brand identity that stands as a testament to your business's values, aspirations, and unwavering commitment to excellence.

Crafting Your Brand Story

In the tapestry of business, your brand story is the narrative thread that weaves together your history, values, and aspirations. This chapter delves into the art of crafting a brand story – a tale that resonates with your audience, fosters emotional connections, and creates a lasting impression. Just as a storyteller captivates an audience, so too must you captivate hearts and minds with a narrative that transcends transactions.

Discovering the Origins

Every brand has a genesis – a starting point that lays the foundation for its journey. Uncover the roots of your business: the passion, inspiration, or problem that led to its creation. Share the anecdotes, struggles, and breakthroughs that shaped your path. These origin stories humanize your brand and foster relatability.

Defining Core Values and Mission

Core values are the compass that guides your brand's decisions and actions. Define the principles that drive your business, shaping its culture and relationships. Align your brand's mission with the positive impact you aspire to make in the world. A well-defined mission not only informs your narrative but also attracts like-minded customers and partners.

Showcasing Customer-Centricity

The heroes of your brand story are not just your products; they are your customers. Highlight how your brand's offerings transform lives, solve problems, or fulfill needs. Share real-life success stories and testimonials that underscore the value your brand brings to your audience.

Weaving Emotional Connections

Emotions are the threads that bind your brand to your audience. Craft your brand story to evoke emotions that resonate with your target audience. Whether it's nostalgia, empathy, or inspiration, infuse your narrative with moments that tug at heartstrings and create lasting memories.

Aligning with Your Audience's Values

Your brand story is a mirror that reflects your audience's aspirations and values. Research and understand the values that resonate with your target demographic.

Craft a narrative that demonstrates how your brand's mission aligns with these shared values, creating a bond that transcends transactions.

Creating Consistency across Channels

Your brand story should sing in harmony across all channels. From your website to social media, ensure that your brand's narrative, tone, and visual elements remain consistent. Consistency builds trust and reinforces your brand's authenticity.

Narrative Evolution: Embracing Change

Your brand story is not static; it evolves as your business grows and adapts. Embrace change while staying true to your brand's essence. Communicate milestones, innovations, and adaptations in a way that aligns with your narrative.

Crafting your brand story is not just about words; it's about weaving an experience that leaves an indelible mark. As you delve into this chapter, remember that your brand story is not just an introduction; it's an invitation to join a journey of shared values, aspirations, and impact. Your mastery of this art transforms your business from a mere entity into a living narrative that resonates with customers, fosters loyalty, and creates a legacy that endures. Just as a bard weaves tales that echo through generations, so too must you weave a brand story that reverberates in the hearts and minds of your audience.

Designing a Memorable Logo and Visual Identity

In the visual realm of business, a well-crafted logo and visual identity serve as the visual signature that encapsulates your brand's essence. This chapter delves into the art of designing a memorable logo and visual identity – a symphony of colors, shapes, and typography that communicates your brand's personality, values, and aspirations. Just as an artist's stroke creates a masterpiece, so too must you design an identity that leaves an indelible mark on the canvas of your industry.

The Essence of a Logo

A logo is not just a symbol; it's the distilled essence of your brand. Reflect on your brand's values, mission, and unique selling proposition. Work with designers to create a logo that encapsulates these elements in a simple, memorable form. Whether it's an abstract emblem, a typographic mark, or a combination, ensure that your logo is versatile and scalable.

Color Palette: Speaking a Visual Language

Colors are the chords that compose your brand's visual melody. Select a color palette that resonates with your brand's personality and aligns with the emotions you want to evoke. Each color carries psychological connotations, so choose wisely. Consistency in color usage across all platforms enhances brand recognition and creates a cohesive visual identity.

Typography: Conveying Tone and Message

Typography is the script that conveys your brand's tone and message. Select fonts that match your brand's personality – whether it's bold and modern or elegant and timeless. Create a hierarchy of fonts for various uses, such as headlines, body text, and calls to action. Consistency in typography maintains visual coherence across all brand touchpoints.

Logo Variations and Usage Guidelines

Your logo is not static; it adapts to various contexts. Design different variations of your logo for different applications – from horizontal to vertical layouts. Develop clear usage guidelines that dictate how your logo should be used, specifying minimum sizes, clear space, and placement on different materials.

Creating Visual Consistency

Visual identity is more than individual elements; it's the symphony they create together. Establish visual consistency by ensuring that your logo, color palette, and typography are used consistently across all brand materials – from your website and social media to business cards and packaging. Consistency breeds recognition and reinforces your brand's professionalism.

Versatility and Scalability

Your visual identity should be versatile and adaptable. Test its effectiveness in various scenarios – from digital screens to print materials. Ensure that your logo and visual elements remain clear and recognizable at different sizes and resolutions.

Evolving with Your Brand

Visual identity is not static; it evolves with your brand's growth and evolution. Periodically evaluate your visual identity to ensure it remains relevant and aligned with your brand's positioning. If your business undergoes a significant transformation, consider refreshing or redesigning your visual elements to reflect the changes.

Designing a memorable logo and visual identity is not just about aesthetics; it's about creating a visual language that communicates your brand's personality, values, and promise. As you delve into this chapter, remember that your logo is not just an image; it's a symbol that embodies the soul of your business. Your mastery of visual identity empowers you to imprint your brand's essence in the minds of your audience, creating a visual journey that evokes emotions, fosters recognition, and tells a story that transcends words. Just as a conductor directs an orchestra, so too must you orchestrate visual elements that

compose a symphony of authenticity,
resonance, and lasting impact.

Establishing Consistent Branding Across Channels

In the dynamic world of business, consistent branding is the thread that weaves together your brand's narrative across every touchpoint. This chapter delves into the art of establishing consistent branding across channels – a strategic endeavor that reinforces your brand's authenticity, fosters recognition, and creates a seamless experience for your audience. Just as a conductor ensures harmony in an orchestra, so too must you orchestrate branding that resonates in unison across all platforms.

The Power of Consistency

Consistency is not just a visual choice; it's a strategic imperative. Your brand's messaging, visual elements, and tone should remain uniform across all channels – from your website and social media to printed materials and in-person interactions. Consistency builds trust, enhances recognition, and solidifies your brand's presence in the minds of your audience.

Creating Brand Guidelines

Brand guidelines are the rulebook that defines how your brand should be presented. These guidelines encompass your logo usage, color palette, typography, tone of voice, and more. Develop comprehensive guidelines that provide clear instructions for anyone creating content or materials on behalf of your brand. Consistent execution ensures that your brand's personality remains intact across all channels.

Digital Presence: Websites and Social Media

Your digital presence is the online manifestation of your brand's identity. Ensure that your website design, color scheme, and typography align with your established visual identity. Carry this consistency to your social media platforms by using the same logo, colors, and tone. This harmonious presentation fosters recognition and a cohesive user experience.

Print Materials: Business Cards, Flyers, and More

Print materials are tangible extensions of your brand. Whether it's business cards, brochures, or flyers, maintain consistency in design elements such as logo placement, color usage, and typography. When recipients encounter your print materials, they should experience the same brand personality they encounter online.

Packaging and Product Design

For businesses with physical products, packaging design is a canvas for your brand identity. Ensure that your packaging aligns with your visual identity, creating a seamless transition from online discovery to unboxing. Consistent packaging design not only enhances brand recognition but also reinforces the quality of your offerings.

In-Person Interactions and Customer Service

Consistency extends beyond the digital realm; it encompasses every touchpoint where your brand interacts with customers. Train your team to embody your brand's tone, values, and customer service principles. Whether it's in-person interactions, customer support, or public events, every engagement should reflect your brand's identity.

Monitoring and Adjusting

Consistency doesn't mean stagnation; it means refinement. Continuously monitor how your brand is being presented across different channels. Regularly review your materials, digital platforms, and customer interactions to ensure alignment with your brand guidelines. Adjust as needed to accommodate new opportunities, industry trends, or changes in your business.

Establishing consistent branding across channels is not a formality; it's a strategic commitment that fosters recognition, trust, and a seamless customer experience. As you delve into this chapter, remember that consistency is not restrictive; it's liberating. Your mastery of this art empowers you to create a symphony of recognition and resonance, where every touchpoint harmonizes to create an authentic, memorable brand experience. Just as a conductor unifies individual musicians into a single performance, so too must you unify your brand's elements to create a harmonious journey that leaves a lasting impression on your audience.

Developing a Marketing Plan

In the strategic landscape of business, a well-crafted marketing plan is the compass that guides your brand toward its goals. This chapter delves into the art of developing a comprehensive marketing plan – a roadmap that aligns your brand's objectives with targeted strategies, channels, and tactics. Just as a navigator plots the course for a voyage, so too must you chart the path that leads to visibility, engagement, and growth.

Setting Clear Objectives

A marketing plan begins with defining clear objectives. Are you aiming to increase brand awareness, boost sales, launch a new product, or expand to new markets?

Objectives provide direction and enable you to measure the effectiveness of your efforts.

Understanding Your Target Audience

Your target audience is the compass that guides your marketing strategies. Analyze their demographics, behaviors, pain points, and preferences. This understanding enables you to tailor your messages, content, and channels to resonate deeply with your audience.

Crafting Key Messages

Key messages are the core statements that communicate your brand's value proposition. Craft messages that succinctly convey what sets your brand apart and how it addresses your audience's needs. These messages become the foundation of your marketing communications.

Choosing the Right Marketing Channels

The marketing landscape is vast, comprising various channels from digital to traditional. Select channels that align with your audience's behaviors and preferences. Whether it's social media, content marketing, email campaigns, or paid advertising, each channel should serve a purpose in reaching your goals.

Content Strategy and Creation

Content is the currency of engagement in the digital age. Develop a content strategy that encompasses blog posts, videos, infographics, and more. Create content that educates, entertains, and resonates with your audience's interests.

Budget Allocation and Resource Planning

Allocate your budget wisely across different marketing activities. Consider factors like advertising costs, content creation, and technology tools. Ensure you have the necessary resources – both financial and human – to execute your plan effectively.

Measuring and Analyzing Results

A successful marketing plan is not a shot in the dark; it's data-driven. Establish metrics to measure the effectiveness of your strategies. Monitor key performance indicators (KPIs) such as website traffic, conversion rates, social engagement, and sales. Regularly analyze the data to determine what's working and what needs adjustment.

Adapting and Optimizing

Flexibility is key in marketing. Based on the insights gained from analyzing results, adapt and optimize your strategies. Be prepared to pivot if certain tactics are not yielding the desired outcomes. Continuous improvement ensures your marketing plan remains aligned with your evolving goals.

Developing a marketing plan is not a static exercise; it's a dynamic process that navigates your brand toward success. As you immerse yourself in this chapter, remember that a well-crafted plan is more than a document; it's a roadmap that guides your brand's journey. Your mastery of this art empowers you to harness the power of strategy, creativity, and data to create a symphony of visibility, engagement, and growth. Just as a conductor shapes the performance of an orchestra, so too must you shape your marketing plan to orchestrate a narrative of impact and transformation.

Creating a Comprehensive Marketing Strategy

In the dynamic landscape of business, a comprehensive marketing strategy is the blueprint that aligns your brand's vision with actionable tactics. This chapter delves into the art of creating a comprehensive marketing strategy – a strategic framework that weaves together objectives, target audiences, channels, and campaigns into a harmonious narrative. Just as an architect designs a structure to withstand the test of time, so too must you design a marketing strategy that propels your brand toward enduring success.

Strategic Alignment and Objectives

Begin by aligning your marketing strategy with your overall business goals. Define specific, measurable, achievable, relevant, and time-bound (SMART) objectives. Whether it's boosting sales by a certain percentage, increasing website traffic, or expanding into new markets, objectives provide clarity and direction.

Deep Audience Understanding

Your audience is at the heart of your marketing strategy. Conduct thorough research to understand their demographics, behaviors, needs, and pain points. Develop detailed buyer personas that guide your messaging and campaigns, ensuring they resonate deeply with your target audience.

Integrated Channels and Tactics

A comprehensive marketing strategy leverages a mix of channels to reach your audience where they are. Blend digital and traditional tactics, such as social media, content marketing, email campaigns, influencer partnerships, and events. Each channel should contribute to a cohesive narrative and support your objectives.

Content as a Pillar

Content is the backbone of modern marketing. Craft a content strategy that addresses your audience's questions, challenges, and interests. Develop a diverse range of content formats – from blog posts and videos to ebooks and webinars – that cater to different stages of the buyer's journey.

Engagement and Interaction

Engagement is not a one-way street; it's a dialogue that fosters connections. Develop strategies to engage your audience on social media, respond to comments and messages, and encourage user-generated content. Create opportunities for meaningful interactions that strengthen brand loyalty.

Campaign Planning and Execution

Campaigns are the stories you tell to captivate your audience's attention. Plan and execute campaigns that align with your objectives and resonate with your audience's emotions. Whether it's a product launch, a seasonal promotion, or a cause-driven initiative, campaigns amplify your brand's presence and impact.

Measurement and Data Analysis

A data-driven strategy is the foundation of success. Identify key performance indicators (KPIs) that align with your objectives. Use analytics tools to track metrics such as website traffic, conversion rates, engagement, and ROI. Regularly analyze data to gauge your strategy's effectiveness and make informed adjustments.

Flexibility and Adaptation

The business landscape is ever-evolving, and your marketing strategy should be adaptable. Regularly review your strategy's performance and make adjustments based on data insights. Be prepared to pivot if market conditions change or new opportunities emerge.

Creating a comprehensive marketing strategy is not a singular event; it's an ongoing journey of strategy, creativity, and adaptation. As you delve into this chapter, remember that a well-crafted strategy is not just a plan; it's a symphony that harmonizes objectives, tactics, and data to create a narrative of growth and impact.

Your mastery of this art empowers you to navigate the currents of change, seize opportunities, and orchestrate a brand journey that resonates with your audience, fosters loyalty, and leaves a lasting legacy. Just as a conductor directs an orchestra, so too must you direct your marketing strategy to create a harmonious narrative that stands as a testament to your brand's vision, innovation, and success.

Leveraging Digital Marketing Channels

In the digital age, marketing transcends boundaries, reaching global audiences with the click of a button. This chapter delves into the art of leveraging digital marketing channels – a strategic pursuit that capitalizes on the power of technology to connect, engage, and convert your target audience. Just as a navigator charts a course through uncharted waters, so too must you navigate the dynamic landscape of digital channels to guide your brand toward visibility and success.

Understanding the Digital Landscape

Digital marketing channels are the avenues that connect your brand with online audiences. Familiarize yourself with the diverse platforms available – from social media and search engines to email marketing, content platforms, and more. Each channel serves a unique purpose and caters to specific audience behaviors.

Search Engine Optimization (SEO)

SEO is the art of climbing search engine ranks to be visible to potential customers. Optimize your website's content, structure, and technical elements to improve its visibility on search engines. Implementing effective SEO strategies enhances your organic visibility and drives targeted traffic to your website.

Content Marketing and Blogging

Content is the heart of digital marketing. Develop a content strategy that addresses your audience's questions, pain points, and interests. Regularly publish valuable blog posts, articles, and other forms of content that establish your brand as an authoritative source in your industry.

Social Media Marketing

Social media platforms are virtual town squares where conversations happen. Choose platforms relevant to your audience and industry, and craft engaging content that sparks conversations, builds relationships, and fosters brand loyalty. Use social media ads to amplify your reach and target specific demographics.

Email Marketing

Email remains a powerful tool for building and nurturing customer relationships. Develop segmented email lists and send personalized messages that provide value to your subscribers. From promotional offers to informative newsletters, email marketing keeps your brand top-of-mind.

Pay-Per-Click (PPC) Advertising

PPC advertising allows you to place targeted ads on search engines and other platforms, paying only when users click on them. Research relevant keywords, create compelling ad copy, and optimize landing pages to drive conversions. PPC campaigns can yield immediate results and boost visibility.

Influencer Marketing

Influencers are the modern word-of-mouth marketers. Collaborate with influencers in your industry to reach their engaged audiences. Choose influencers whose values align with your brand and whose followers match your target demographic.

Video Marketing

Video is a dynamic format that captures attention and conveys messages effectively. Create engaging video content, such as explainer videos, tutorials, product demonstrations, and behind-the-scenes glimpses. Share videos on platforms like YouTube, social media, and your website.

Analytics and Data Insights

The digital realm is abundant with data that provides insights into your audience's behaviors and preferences. Utilize analytics tools to track website traffic, engagement, conversions, and other key metrics. Regularly analyze the data to optimize your strategies and make informed decisions.

Leveraging digital marketing channels is not just about mastering technology; it's about crafting compelling narratives that resonate in the online realm. As you immerse yourself in this chapter, remember that digital channels are more than tools; they are platforms for engagement, connection, and impact. Your mastery of this art empowers you to navigate the dynamic landscape of the digital world, creating a symphony of visibility, engagement, and growth. Just as a navigator steers a ship through unpredictable waters, so too must you navigate digital channels to guide your brand toward success and recognition in the vast ocean of the online world.

Exploring Traditional Marketing Methods

In the ever-evolving landscape of marketing, traditional methods remain steadfast as pillars of brand promotion. This chapter delves into the art of exploring traditional marketing methods – a strategic endeavor that combines time-tested techniques with modern innovations to create a well-rounded approach to reaching your target audience. Just as an architect blends classic design elements with modern aesthetics, so too must you blend traditional methods with contemporary insights to craft a comprehensive marketing strategy.

Print Advertising

Print advertising includes avenues like newspapers, magazines, brochures, and flyers. Craft visually appealing ads that communicate your brand's value proposition concisely. Consider your audience's reading habits and preferences to choose the most relevant print mediums.

Direct Mail Marketing

Direct mail delivers tangible messages to your audience's doorstep. Create personalized mailers that resonate with recipients' interests and needs. Incorporate compelling visuals and engaging copy to make your direct mail pieces stand out in the mailbox.

Television and Radio Advertising

Broadcast media remains a powerful way to reach mass audiences. Craft engaging TV and radio commercials that capture attention and deliver your brand message effectively. Target specific time slots and channels that align with your audience demographics.

Outdoor Advertising

Billboards, bus stop posters, and signage offer a visual presence in the physical world. Design eye-catching visuals and concise messaging that can be absorbed quickly by passersby. Choose locations strategically to maximize visibility among your target audience.

Event Marketing and Sponsorships

Participating in or sponsoring events offers an opportunity for face-to-face engagement. Choose events that align with your brand's values and appeal to your target demographic. Use event marketing to build relationships, showcase products, and create memorable experiences.

Networking and Word-of-Mouth

Networking remains a potent tool for relationship-building. Attend industry events, trade shows, and business gatherings to establish connections and promote your brand. Word-of-mouth referrals from satisfied customers can also drive organic growth.

Public Relations (PR)

PR is the art of managing your brand's reputation and visibility. Craft compelling press releases, pitch stories to the media, and engage with journalists. Positive media coverage enhances your brand's credibility and exposure.

Branded Promotional Items

Branded promotional items serve as tangible reminders of your brand. Distribute items like pens, keychains, or tote bags that showcase your logo and messaging. These items can leave a lasting impression and foster brand recognition.

Combining Traditional and Digital

The synergy between traditional and digital marketing is a powerful strategy. For example, you can use QR codes on print materials to drive audiences to your website or social media profiles. Combining traditional methods with digital touchpoints enhances engagement and bridges the gap between offline and online interactions.

Exploring traditional marketing methods is not about rejecting the new; it's about embracing the timeless. As you delve into this chapter, remember that traditional methods are not relics; they are foundational elements that, when combined with modern insights, create a comprehensive marketing strategy. Your mastery of this art empowers you to harmonize the familiar with the innovative, creating a symphony of brand visibility, engagement, and impact. Just as an artist blends classic techniques with contemporary flair, so too must you blend traditional methods with digital prowess to craft a marketing strategy that stands as a testament to your brand's versatility, authenticity, and enduring success.

Enhancing Your Product or Service Offering

In the dynamic realm of business, continuous improvement is the catalyst for growth and customer loyalty. This chapter delves into the art of enhancing your product or service offering – a strategic pursuit that involves innovation, customer-centricity, and a commitment to delivering exceptional value. Just as a craftsman refines their masterpiece, so too must you refine your offerings to exceed customer expectations and stand out in the market.

Listening to Customer Feedback

Your customers are a wellspring of insights. Listen attentively to their feedback, both positive and constructive. Understand their pain points, desires, and suggestions. This feedback serves as a compass for your enhancements.

Identifying Pain Points and Needs

Successful enhancements address specific pain points or fulfill unmet needs. Analyze customer behavior, reviews, and industry trends to pinpoint areas where your offering can be improved. A deep understanding of your customers' challenges guides your innovation.

Innovation and Adaptation

Innovation is the fuel of progress. Introduce new features, functionalities, or improvements that align with customer preferences and technological advancements. Whether it's enhancing product performance, adding new services, or simplifying processes, innovation keeps your offering relevant.

Quality and Performance Optimization

Enhancements should always focus on quality. Strive to exceed expectations in terms of durability, usability, and performance. Quality improvements not only satisfy existing customers but also attract new ones through positive word-of-mouth.

Personalization and Customization

Tailoring your offering to individual customer preferences enhances their experience. Introduce options for customization, allowing customers to choose features or services that suit their specific needs. Personalization fosters a sense of ownership and loyalty.

Adding Value through Bundling

Bundle complementary products or services to provide added value. This approach encourages customers to explore more of what you offer and enhances their overall satisfaction. Bundles can also provide cost savings, making them an attractive proposition.

Education and Support

Enhancements should be accompanied by education and support. Provide clear instructions, tutorials, or documentation to guide customers through new features.

Robust customer support ensures a smooth transition and reinforces your commitment to their success.

Feedback Loop and Continuous Improvement

The process of enhancement is iterative. Create a feedback loop that encourages ongoing communication with customers. Regularly assess the impact of your enhancements, gather feedback, and refine your offerings accordingly.

Maintaining Competitive Edge

Enhancements are not just about meeting expectations; they're about staying ahead of the competition. Continuously monitor the market and stay attuned to emerging trends.

Strive to set new standards that differentiate your brand.

Enhancing your product or service offering is not a one-time effort; it's a continuous commitment to excellence. As you immerse yourself in this chapter, remember that enhancements are not just about features; they're about customer value. Your mastery of this art empowers you to craft offerings that delight, exceed expectations, and create a legacy of customer loyalty. Just as an artisan hones their craft to perfection, so too must you refine your offerings to stand as a testament to your brand's dedication to innovation, quality, and enduring success.

Gathering Customer Feedback

In the intricate realm of business, customer feedback is the compass that guides your decisions and shapes your brand's evolution. This chapter delves into the art of gathering customer feedback – a strategic endeavor that involves active listening, empathy, and a commitment to understanding your audience's needs and desires. Just as a keen observer absorbs the nuances of their surroundings, so too must you gather insights to refine your offerings and foster lasting relationships.

The Value of Customer Feedback

Customer feedback is a treasure trove of insights. It reveals what's working, what needs improvement, and what opportunities exist. This knowledge empowers you to make informed decisions, enhance your products or services, and deliver a superior customer experience.

Creating Feedback Channels

Provide accessible channels for customers to voice their opinions. This can include surveys, feedback forms on your website, social media polls, customer reviews, and direct communication through email or phone. Offering multiple avenues ensures you capture feedback from various touchpoints.

Listening Actively and Empathetically

Listening is more than just hearing; it's understanding. When customers share their feedback, listen actively and empathize with their perspective. Acknowledge their experiences, challenges, and suggestions, demonstrating your commitment to their satisfaction.

Surveys and Questionnaires

Structured surveys and questionnaires allow you to gather specific insights. Craft questions that address various aspects of your business – from product usability and customer service to overall satisfaction. Keep surveys concise to encourage higher response rates.

Online Reviews and Ratings

Online reviews and ratings are windows into customer experiences. Monitor review platforms and respond to both positive and negative feedback. Positive feedback can be celebrated, while negative feedback presents opportunities for improvement.

Feedback from Customer Interactions

Interactions with customers provide invaluable real-time feedback. Pay attention to their inquiries, comments, and concerns. These interactions reveal immediate insights into pain points and opportunities for improvement.

Social Media Listening

Social media platforms are virtual spaces where conversations about your brand unfold. Use social media monitoring tools to track mentions, comments, and discussions related to your business. Engage with users and address their feedback proactively.

Employee Feedback

Your frontline employees interact directly with customers. Encourage them to gather feedback during these interactions. They can relay valuable insights, identify trends, and contribute to your understanding of customer sentiment.

Data Analysis and Trends

Collecting feedback is not enough; you must analyze the data. Look for trends, patterns, and recurring themes in customer feedback. This analysis provides a deeper understanding of overarching issues and opportunities.

Continuous Improvement

Feedback is a catalyst for growth. Use the insights gathered to refine your offerings, processes, and strategies. Show your customers that their feedback leads to tangible improvements, fostering a sense of partnership and loyalty.

Gathering customer feedback is not just about data collection; it's about building bridges of understanding and partnership. As you immerse yourself in this chapter, remember that customer feedback is not just information; it's an opportunity for growth. Your mastery of this art empowers you to create a feedback loop that fosters relationships, drives innovation, and fuels a culture of customer-centricity. Just as an attentive listener absorbs the nuances of a story, so too must you absorb the insights your customers share to refine your offerings and create a brand journey that resonates with their needs and aspirations.

Innovating and Iterating Your Products/Services

In the ever-evolving landscape of business, innovation is the compass that guides your brand toward growth and relevance. This chapter delves into the art of innovating and iterating your products or services – a strategic pursuit that involves creativity, adaptability, and a commitment to staying ahead of the curve. Just as an artist continually refines their masterpiece, so too must you refine your offerings to meet changing customer needs and market demands.

Embracing a Culture of Innovation

Innovation begins with a mindset. Foster a culture where creativity is encouraged, risks are embraced, and the status quo is constantly questioned. Cultivate an environment where team members feel empowered to propose and explore new ideas.

Identifying Emerging Trends

Stay attuned to industry trends and emerging technologies. Continuously monitor market shifts, customer preferences, and advancements that could impact your industry. Being proactive in identifying trends positions your brand as a thought leader.

Listening to Customer Needs

Your customers are a wellspring of inspiration. Engage in active listening to understand their evolving needs, challenges, and aspirations. This understanding serves as a foundation for innovation that directly addresses their pain points.

Iterative Improvement

Iteration is the key to refinement. Continuously evaluate your products or services based on customer feedback, data analysis, and performance metrics. Make incremental improvements that enhance usability, features, and overall value.

Research and Development (R&D)

Invest in research and development to explore new possibilities. Allocate resources to experiment with new technologies, features, or enhancements that can elevate your offerings. R&D fuels your brand's capacity to innovate.

Prototyping and Testing

Before a full-scale launch, prototype and test your innovations. This process helps identify potential flaws, gather feedback, and make necessary adjustments. Prototyping minimizes risks associated with introducing new elements.

Collaboration and Cross-Functional Teams

Innovation thrives in collaborative environments. Create cross-functional teams that bring together diverse perspectives and expertise. Collaborative efforts often lead to novel ideas and holistic solutions.

Beta Testing and User Feedback

Invite a select group of customers to participate in beta testing. Their firsthand experiences and feedback provide insights into how your innovations are received and used. Beta testing allows you to fine-tune your offerings before a wider release.

Risk Management and Learning from Failure

Innovation inherently involves risk. Embrace a mindset that views failure as a stepping stone to success. When an innovation doesn't meet expectations, analyze the reasons for its shortcomings and apply those lessons to future endeavors.

Incorporating Sustainable Practices

Innovation extends beyond features; it includes sustainability. Explore ways to integrate eco-friendly practices, materials, or processes into your products or services. A commitment to sustainability aligns with changing consumer values.

Innovating and iterating your products or services is not just about staying current; it's about leading the way. As you delve into this chapter, remember that innovation is not just an event; it's a continuous pursuit. Your mastery of this art empowers you to push boundaries, embrace change, and craft offerings that resonate with the evolving needs of your audience. Just as an inventor refines their creation through multiple iterations, so too must you refine your products or services to create a brand journey that stands as a testament to your brand's commitment to innovation, excellence, and enduring success.

Adding Value through Features and Benefits

In the intricate realm of business, adding value is the cornerstone of building strong customer relationships and brand loyalty. This chapter delves into the art of adding value through features and benefits – a strategic endeavor that involves understanding customer needs, crafting meaningful enhancements, and communicating how your offerings can positively impact their lives. Just as a sculptor adds intricate details to their creation, so too must you add features and benefits that enrich the customer experience.

Understanding Customer Needs

The foundation of value addition is empathy. Understand your customers' pain points, desires, and aspirations. Identify gaps in their journey that your products or services can address. This understanding guides your value-enhancing efforts.

Features: Enhancing Functionality

Features are the building blocks that enhance the functionality of your offerings. Develop features that solve problems, streamline processes, or introduce new capabilities. Each feature should have a clear purpose and align with customer needs.

Benefits: Solving Problems

Benefits are the positive outcomes that customers gain from using your product or service. Clearly communicate how your features translate into benefits that solve their challenges or fulfill their desires. Focus on the transformational impact.

Personalization and Customization

Empower customers to tailor your offerings to their preferences. Introduce options for personalization and customization that resonate with their unique needs. Personalized experiences foster a sense of ownership and loyalty.

Simplicity and User-Friendly Design

Simplicity is a powerful form of value. Design your offerings with user-friendliness in mind. Intuitive interfaces, clear instructions, and easy navigation enhance the customer experience and reduce friction.

Educational Resources

Value extends beyond the product or service itself. Provide educational resources that empower customers to maximize their experience. This can include tutorials, guides, webinars, and other materials that help them derive full value.

Time-Saving Solutions

Time is a valuable resource. If your offerings can save customers time, emphasize this benefit. Highlight how your products or services streamline processes, automate tasks, or simplify complex workflows.

Quality and Durability

High-quality offerings contribute to long-term value. Invest in quality materials, craftsmanship, and durability. A product or service that stands the test of time enhances customer satisfaction and loyalty.

Cost Savings and Return on Investment (ROI)

Demonstrate how your offerings deliver cost savings or a positive ROI. Whether it's through increased efficiency, reduced expenses, or improved outcomes, showcasing financial benefits resonates with customers.

Solving Pain Points

Value often lies in solving specific pain points. Identify the challenges your customers face and emphasize how your offerings alleviate those pains. This approach resonates deeply with their needs.

Adding value through features and benefits is not just about enhancements; it's about enriching lives. As you immerse yourself in this chapter, remember that value is not just about what you offer; it's about how you impact your customers' world. Your mastery of this art empowers you to create a narrative of transformation, empathy, and enduring satisfaction. Just as an architect designs a building to cater to its occupants' needs, so too must you design your offerings to cater to your customers' needs, leaving a lasting impression that speaks to the meaningful impact your brand makes.

Optimizing Operations for Growth

In the intricate dance of business, efficient operations form the foundation for sustainable growth. This chapter delves into the art of optimizing operations – a strategic pursuit that involves streamlining processes, leveraging technology, and fostering a culture of continuous improvement. Just as a conductor harmonizes individual musicians to create a symphony, so too must you orchestrate your operations to create a harmonious journey toward success.

Streamlining Processes

Efficiency begins with well-defined processes. Analyze your workflows to identify bottlenecks, redundancies, and areas of improvement. Streamline processes to eliminate waste, reduce delays, and enhance productivity.

Leveraging Technology

Technology is a catalyst for efficiency. Embrace tools and software that automate tasks, improve collaboration, and provide real-time insights. From project management platforms to customer relationship management systems, technology optimizes your operations.

Employee Training and Development

Invest in your team's skills and knowledge. Provide training that equips employees with the tools to excel in their roles. A skilled and motivated workforce enhances productivity and contributes to a positive work environment.

Data-Driven Decision-Making

Harness the power of data to guide your decisions. Collect and analyze data related to your operations, customer behavior, and market trends. Data-driven insights help you make informed choices that drive growth.

Supply Chain Optimization

If your business involves physical products, optimize your supply chain. Ensure efficient procurement, inventory management, and distribution processes. A well-organized supply chain minimizes costs and ensures timely deliveries.

Customer Relationship Management (CRM)

A robust CRM system is essential for managing customer interactions. Use CRM tools to track customer inquiries, sales leads, and service requests. A centralized system enhances customer communication and relationship management.

Quality Assurance and Control

Maintain high-quality standards across your offerings. Implement quality control processes to ensure consistent products or services. Quality assurance builds trust and fosters customer satisfaction.

Agility and Adaptability

In a rapidly changing landscape, agility is a competitive advantage. Create a culture of adaptability that allows your team to respond quickly to market shifts, customer feedback, and emerging opportunities.

Continuous Improvement

Optimization is an ongoing journey. Foster a culture of continuous improvement where team members actively contribute ideas for refining processes. Encourage regular assessments and adjustments.

Scaling Strategies

As you optimize, consider scalability. Plan strategies that accommodate growth without compromising efficiency. Whether it's expanding your workforce, diversifying your offerings, or entering new markets, scalability is a strategic consideration.

Optimizing operations is not just about efficiency; it's about setting the stage for growth. As you delve into this chapter, remember that optimization is not a destination; it's a journey. Your mastery of this art empowers you to create a symphony of efficiency, innovation, and lasting impact.

Just as a choreographer designs routines to showcase the dancers' skills, so too must you design your operations to showcase your team's capabilities, enabling them to perform at their best and driving your business toward sustained success and growth.

Streamlining Business Processes

In the intricate tapestry of business, streamlined processes are the thread that weaves efficiency and productivity into the fabric of success. This chapter delves into the art of streamlining business processes – a strategic pursuit that involves identifying inefficiencies, optimizing workflows, and creating a seamless foundation for growth. Just as an architect designs a space for optimal functionality, so too must you design your processes to maximize effectiveness and achieve your business objectives.

Process Mapping and Analysis

Begin by mapping out your existing processes. Visualize each step, decision point, and handoff involved. Analyze these maps to identify bottlenecks, redundancies, and areas where improvements can be made.

Identifying Inefficiencies

Spotlight inefficiencies that hinder productivity and waste resources. Look for tasks that take longer than necessary, unnecessary manual steps, or frequent delays. These inefficiencies provide opportunities for enhancement.

Standardizing Procedures

Standardization promotes consistency and reduces errors. Develop standardized procedures and guidelines for routine tasks. This clarity ensures that everyone follows best practices, minimizing confusion and improving outcomes.

Automation and Technology Integration

Leverage technology to automate repetitive tasks and manual processes. Implement software and tools that handle routine functions, freeing up human resources for more strategic activities. Automation enhances efficiency and reduces errors.

Eliminating Redundancies

Identify redundant processes that create unnecessary work. Streamline by consolidating steps, eliminating duplicate efforts, and optimizing resource allocation. Reducing redundancies reduces wasted time and resources.

Clear Communication and Collaboration

Efficient processes hinge on clear communication and collaboration. Establish streamlined communication channels and platforms that facilitate information sharing and decision-making. Effective collaboration minimizes delays and misunderstandings.

Empowering Employees

Involve your team in process optimization. Encourage them to contribute ideas for improvement based on their day-to-day experiences. Empowered employees are more likely to proactively identify areas for enhancement.

Continuous Monitoring and Improvement

Streamlining is an ongoing effort. Regularly monitor the effectiveness of your streamlined processes. Collect feedback from team members and stakeholders to identify any emerging issues or new opportunities for improvement.

Metrics and Key Performance Indicators (KPIs)

Use metrics and KPIs to measure process efficiency. Track factors such as cycle time, resource utilization, and error rates. Data-driven insights provide a clear view of the impact of your streamlining efforts.

Training and Onboarding

Efficient processes are most effective when everyone understands and follows them. Ensure proper training and onboarding for new team members to ensure consistent adherence to streamlined procedures.

Streamlining business processes is not just about efficiency; it's about creating a foundation for growth. As you delve into this chapter, remember that streamlining is not a one-time event; it's a continuous pursuit. Your mastery of this art empowers you to create a symphony of efficiency, collaboration, and innovation. Just as a choreographer designs a routine for flawless execution, so too must you design your processes to ensure that your business moves seamlessly toward its goals, powered by a harmonious interplay of optimized workflows and strategic foresight.

Improving Efficiency and Productivity

In the dynamic landscape of business, efficiency and productivity are the engines that drive success and growth. This chapter delves into the art of improving efficiency and productivity – a strategic pursuit that involves optimizing workflows, fostering a culture of effectiveness, and maximizing the output of your resources. Just as a conductor orchestrates the musicians to create a harmonious symphony, so too must you orchestrate your operations to create a symphony of efficiency and achievement.

Process Assessment and Analysis

Begin by assessing your existing processes. Analyze each step, resource allocation, and potential bottlenecks. Identify areas where efficiency can be improved through streamlined procedures and reduced waste.

Goal Setting and Prioritization

Set clear objectives and prioritize tasks based on their importance and alignment with your business goals. Clear goals provide a roadmap for your team's efforts and focus their energy on high-impact activities.

Time Management and Task Allocation

Effective time management is pivotal. Allocate time blocks for different tasks and avoid multitasking, which can lead to reduced productivity. Focus on one task at a time to ensure quality and efficiency.

Eliminating Distractions

Distractions can hinder productivity. Create an environment that minimizes interruptions and distractions. Implement strategies such as setting specific work hours, silencing notifications, and dedicating focused work periods.

Automation and Technology Integration

Leverage technology to automate repetitive tasks and streamline workflows. Integrate software and tools that handle routine functions, freeing up valuable human resources for more strategic tasks.

Effective Communication

Clear communication is essential for productivity. Foster transparent and open lines of communication within your team. Ensure that expectations, goals, and feedback are communicated effectively to avoid misunderstandings.

Delegation and Empowerment

Delegating tasks empowers your team and enhances productivity. Assign tasks based on team members' strengths and expertise. Empowered employees take ownership and are more motivated to excel.

Continuous Learning and Skill Development

Invest in skill development for your team. Continuous learning enhances their capabilities, making them more efficient and adaptable. Encourage a culture of learning and provide opportunities for growth.

Feedback and Performance Evaluation

Regular feedback and performance evaluations keep everyone aligned and accountable. Provide constructive feedback to identify areas for improvement and recognize achievements. Clear feedback guides the pursuit of higher efficiency.

Wellness and Work-Life Balance

Efficiency is tied to well-being. Promote a healthy work-life balance and provide resources that support the physical and mental well-being of your team. A balanced lifestyle enhances productivity and creativity.

Improving efficiency and productivity is not just about working harder; it's about working smarter. As you delve into this chapter, remember that efficiency is not a destination; it's a continuous journey. Your mastery of this art empowers you to create a symphony of focus, innovation, and achievement. Just as a conductor guides musicians to create a masterpiece, so too must you guide your team to perform at their best, harmonizing their efforts to achieve greater productivity and success.

Scaling Up Without Compromising Quality

In the intricate realm of business, scaling up is a testament to your brand's growth and potential. This chapter delves into the art of scaling up without compromising quality – a strategic pursuit that involves expanding operations, reaching new markets, and maintaining the high standards that define your brand. Just as an architect designs an extension that seamlessly integrates with the original structure, so too must you scale up while preserving the essence of your brand's excellence.

Preserving Core Values

Maintain your brand's core values as you scale. Your values are the compass that guides decisions and shapes your brand's identity. Ensure that your expansion aligns with these values, creating a consistent and authentic experience.

Scalable Systems and Processes

Design systems and processes that can scale without strain. Streamline workflows, implement efficient procedures, and leverage technology to handle increased demand. Scalable operations ensure quality is not compromised.

Team Alignment and Training

As you scale, ensure your team is aligned with your quality standards. Provide thorough training and clear communication about expectations. A cohesive team that understands and embraces your brand's values upholds quality.

Quality Assurance Protocols

Establish rigorous quality assurance protocols. Regularly assess your offerings to ensure they meet your established standards. This commitment to quality is non-negotiable, regardless of the scale of your operations.

Supplier and Partner Selection

Choose suppliers and partners that share your commitment to quality. Vet potential collaborators thoroughly to ensure they align with your standards. A strong network contributes to maintaining quality throughout expansion.

Feedback-Driven Improvements

Use customer feedback to drive improvements as you scale. Continuous feedback loops help you identify areas where adjustments are needed. Customer insights keep quality at the forefront of your expansion.

Focus on Customer Experience

Scaling should enhance the customer experience. Consider how your expansion impacts customer satisfaction, from increased response times to the availability of support. A positive customer experience upholds quality.

Adaptability and Flexibility

Be prepared to adapt your processes as you scale. While maintaining quality, be open to refining procedures to accommodate increased volume and changing market dynamics.

Monitoring and Measurement

Establish metrics to measure quality throughout your expansion. Track key performance indicators that reflect quality standards, customer satisfaction, and any deviations from your set benchmarks.

Continuous Communication

Communication is key as you scale. Ensure that everyone involved – from your team to customers – is informed about the changes and how they align with your brand's commitment to quality.

Scaling up without compromising quality is not just about expansion; it's about evolution. As you immerse yourself in this chapter, remember that quality is the bedrock of your brand's reputation. Your mastery of this art empowers you to create a symphony of growth, integrity, and excellence. Just as a composer orchestrates harmonious melodies, so too must you orchestrate your expansion to create a seamless blend of growth and quality, ensuring that your brand's reputation for excellence remains untarnished as it expands its horizons.

Financial Planning and Management

In the complex landscape of business, financial prowess is the cornerstone of sustainable success. This chapter delves into the art of financial planning and management – a strategic pursuit that involves budgeting, forecasting, optimizing resources, and making informed decisions to ensure your business's fiscal health. Just as a conductor orchestrates instruments to create a harmonious melody, so too must you orchestrate your finances to create a symphony of stability and growth.

Budgeting and Forecasting

Develop a comprehensive budget that outlines your income, expenses, and financial goals. Forecast future financial scenarios based on market trends and historical data. Budgeting and forecasting guide your financial decisions.

Cash Flow Management

Cash flow is the lifeblood of your business. Monitor and manage cash inflows and outflows to ensure smooth operations. Cash flow analysis helps you identify potential gaps and take proactive measures.

Financial Analysis and Performance Metrics

Regularly analyze financial statements and performance metrics. These insights offer a clear view of your business's financial health. Metrics such as profitability ratios, liquidity ratios, and return on investment guide your decisions.

Debt Management and Financing

Strategically manage debt and financing options. Evaluate interest rates, repayment terms, and the impact of debt on your cash flow. Seek financing avenues that align with your growth goals.

Risk Assessment and Management

Identify potential financial risks and create strategies to mitigate them. Consider scenarios such as economic downturns, market shifts, or changes in customer behavior. Risk management safeguards your business's financial stability.

Cost Control and Optimization

Optimize expenses without compromising quality. Review all costs regularly to identify areas where savings can be achieved. Cost control enhances profitability and ensures resource allocation aligns with strategic goals.

Investment and Growth Strategies

Make informed decisions about investments and growth initiatives. Assess opportunities based on potential returns, risks, and alignment with your business objectives. Sound investment strategies fuel expansion.

Tax Planning and Compliance

Develop tax strategies that minimize liabilities while ensuring compliance with regulations. Proper tax planning can result in significant savings and prevent unexpected financial setbacks.

Contingency Planning

Create contingency plans for unforeseen financial challenges. Establish reserves or emergency funds to navigate unexpected expenses or disruptions in revenue. Contingency planning provides a safety net.

Regular Financial Reviews

Schedule regular financial reviews to assess progress against your goals and make necessary adjustments. These reviews keep your financial strategies aligned with your business's evolving needs.

Financial planning and management is not just about numbers; it's about orchestrating the financial elements of your business for success. As you delve into this chapter, remember that financial acumen is the conductor that guides your business's symphony. Your mastery of this art empowers you to create a harmonious blend of fiscal stability and growth, ensuring that your business thrives in the ever-changing landscape. Just as a conductor guides the musicians to create a masterpiece, so too must you guide your business's financial journey, orchestrating the resources to create a symphony of prosperity and enduring success.

Budgeting for Growth Initiatives

In the dynamic world of business, growth initiatives are the vehicles that propel your brand toward new horizons. This chapter delves into the art of budgeting for growth initiatives – a strategic pursuit that involves allocating resources, forecasting expenses, and ensuring that your business's expansion is both financially prudent and strategically sound. Just as an architect designs a blueprint for a new structure, so too must you design a budget that lays the foundation for successful growth.

Clarify Growth Objectives

Begin by defining your growth objectives. Whether it's entering new markets, launching new products, or expanding your customer base, articulate your goals clearly. These objectives serve as guideposts for your budgeting efforts.

Market Research and Analysis

Conduct thorough market research to estimate the potential costs and benefits of your growth initiatives. Understand the competitive landscape, customer demand, and potential risks. Research provides a realistic basis for your budget.

Cost Identification

Identify all potential costs associated with your growth initiatives. This includes direct expenses such as marketing, research, development, and operational expansion. Additionally, consider indirect costs that may arise as a result of the growth.

Resource Allocation

Allocate resources strategically based on your growth priorities. Determine how much funding will be directed to each initiative. Resource allocation ensures that your budget aligns with your growth goals.

Financial Projections

Forecast the financial impact of your growth initiatives over a specified period. Estimate potential revenues, costs, and profitability. Financial projections guide your budgeting decisions and help assess the feasibility of your plans.

Risk Assessment and Contingencies

Identify potential risks that could impact your growth initiatives. Build contingencies into your budget to address unforeseen challenges. Contingency planning ensures that unexpected hurdles do not derail your plans.

Return on Investment (ROI) Analysis

Evaluate the expected ROI for each growth initiative. Calculate the potential returns relative to the costs involved. ROI analysis helps prioritize initiatives that offer the highest potential for profitability.

Phased Budgeting

Consider phasing your budget based on the stages of your growth initiatives. Break down expenses into phases, aligning with project milestones. Phased budgeting allows for more accurate tracking and adjustments.

Monitoring and Review

Regularly monitor your budget against actual expenses and outcomes. Review financial reports to ensure that your growth initiatives remain on track and make necessary adjustments if deviations occur.

Flexibility and Adjustment

Maintain flexibility in your budgeting approach. As your growth initiatives unfold, be prepared to adjust your budget based on real-time data, market changes, and unexpected developments.

Communication and Alignment

Ensure that key stakeholders are aligned with the budgeting decisions for your growth initiatives. Transparent communication helps secure support and resources for successful execution.

Budgeting for growth initiatives is not just about numbers; it's about strategically funding your business's evolution. As you immerse yourself in this chapter, remember that your budget is the blueprint that guides your expansion. Your mastery of this art empowers you to create a symphony of calculated risk-taking, strategic allocation, and informed decision-making. Just as an architect designs a structure to stand the test of time, so too must you design a budget that supports the growth of your business, ensuring that every resource is allocated to create a harmonious melody of progress and success.

Securing Funding for Expansion

In the dynamic landscape of business, securing funding is the bridge that connects your growth aspirations with practical execution. This chapter delves into the art of securing funding for expansion – a strategic pursuit that involves identifying funding sources, crafting compelling proposals, and navigating the financial landscape to fuel your business's growth. Just as a navigator charts a course to uncharted waters, so too must you navigate the funding landscape to chart a successful path toward expansion.

Assess Funding Needs

Begin by assessing the funding requirements for your expansion plans. Calculate the costs associated with initiatives such as market entry, product development, operational scaling, and marketing. A clear understanding of your financial needs is essential.

Internal Funding Sources

Consider utilizing internal sources of funding. This may include reinvesting profits, tapping into retained earnings, or reallocating existing resources. Internal funding can provide a solid foundation for growth.

Equity Financing

Equity financing involves raising funds by selling shares of your company to investors. This can include venture capital, angel investors, or private equity firms. Be prepared to relinquish a portion of ownership in exchange for capital.

Debt Financing

Debt financing involves borrowing funds that you agree to repay with interest over time. This can include bank loans, lines of credit, or bonds. Assess your ability to service debt and manage repayment obligations.

Crowdfunding

Leverage crowdfunding platforms to raise funds from a large number of individuals. Crowdfunding can be a way to validate your business idea while securing funds for specific projects or initiatives.

Government Grants and Subsidies

Explore government grants and subsidies that support specific industries or initiatives. Research eligibility criteria and application processes to secure financial support from government programs.

Strategic Partnerships and Alliances

Form strategic partnerships with other businesses that can provide funding, resources, or expertise in exchange for shared benefits. Strategic alliances can facilitate growth without solely relying on external funding.

Pitching to Investors

Craft a compelling pitch that outlines your growth plans, market opportunity, competitive advantage, and expected returns. Tailor your pitch to the preferences of potential investors, whether they're angel investors, venture capitalists, or other funding sources.

Business Plan and Financial Projections

Develop a comprehensive business plan that details your expansion strategy, target market, competitive analysis, and financial projections. A well-structured business plan demonstrates your readiness and strategic thinking to potential investors.

Due Diligence and Transparency

Be prepared for due diligence inquiries from potential investors. Provide transparent and accurate information about your business's financials, operations, and growth projections. Transparency builds trust.

Negotiating Terms

Negotiate funding terms that align with your business's interests and growth plans. Consider factors such as equity ownership, interest rates, repayment terms, and exit strategies.

Securing funding for expansion is not just about acquiring capital; it's about aligning financial resources with your growth vision. As you delve into this chapter, remember that securing funding is a strategic endeavor that requires preparation, persuasion, and persistence. Your mastery of this art empowers you to navigate the financial landscape with confidence, creating a symphony of growth and opportunity. Just as a navigator charts a course through uncharted waters, so too must you navigate the funding landscape to steer your business toward new horizons of expansion and success.

Monitoring Financial Performance

In the intricate world of business, monitoring financial performance is the compass that guides your journey toward success. This chapter delves into the art of monitoring financial performance – a strategic pursuit that involves tracking key indicators, analyzing trends, and making informed decisions to ensure your business's fiscal health and growth trajectory. Just as a navigator assesses the stars to guide a ship's course, so too must you assess financial data to steer your business toward prosperity.

Key Performance Indicators (KPIs)

Identify and track relevant KPIs that reflect your business's financial health. Common

KPIs include profitability ratios, liquidity ratios, gross margin, and return on investment. These metrics offer a snapshot of your business's performance.

Financial Statements

Regularly review and analyze financial statements such as income statements, balance sheets, and cash flow statements. These statements provide insights into your business's revenue, expenses, assets, liabilities, and cash flow.

Budget vs. Actual Analysis

Compare actual financial performance against your budgeted projections. This analysis helps you identify areas where you've exceeded or fallen short of expectations. Adjust your strategies based on these findings.

Trend Analysis

Analyze trends in your financial data over time. Look for patterns, growth trajectories, and potential fluctuations. Trend analysis helps you identify opportunities and potential challenges.

Variance Analysis

Understand the reasons behind variations between expected and actual financial performance. Identify factors that contribute to positive or negative variances. This analysis guides corrective actions.

Cash Flow Management

Monitor your cash flow closely. Track inflows and outflows to ensure that your business has sufficient liquidity to meet financial obligations. Cash flow management is crucial for ongoing operations and growth initiatives.

Customer and Product Analysis

Analyze the financial performance of different customer segments or product lines. Identify which areas contribute the most to your revenue and profitability. This analysis guides resource allocation and strategic decisions.

Break-Even Analysis

Calculate your business's break-even point – the level of sales at which revenue equals costs. This analysis helps you understand the minimum sales needed to cover expenses and achieve profitability.

Industry Benchmarking

Compare your financial performance to industry benchmarks. This provides context for evaluating your business's standing within the broader market. Benchmarking highlights areas where improvement is needed.

Scenario Planning

Create scenarios to model potential financial outcomes based on various variables. This exercise helps you prepare for different situations and make proactive decisions to navigate changes in the market.

Monitoring financial performance is not just about numbers; it's about steering your business toward its goals. As you immerse yourself in this chapter, remember that your financial data is a map that guides your decisions. Your mastery of this art empowers you to create a symphony of foresight, strategy, and adaptability. Just as a navigator assesses the stars to guide a ship's course, so too must you assess your financial data to navigate your business toward sustained growth, aligning your actions with the rhythm of success.

Building a Strong Online Presence

In the digital landscape of business, an online presence is the virtual storefront that welcomes customers and connects your brand to the world. This chapter delves into the art of building a strong online presence – a strategic pursuit that involves creating a compelling digital identity, leveraging various online platforms, and engaging with your audience to foster meaningful connections. Just as an artist meticulously crafts a masterpiece, so too must you craft your online presence to captivate and engage your audience.

Defining Your Digital Identity

Begin by defining your brand's digital identity. This includes your brand's personality, values, and voice. Align your online presence with your offline brand identity to create a consistent and authentic experience.

Website Development

Create a user-friendly and visually appealing website that showcases your products or services. Ensure that your website is mobile-responsive, easy to navigate, and optimized for search engines (SEO).

Content Creation and Strategy

Develop a content strategy that provides value to your audience. Create high-quality content such as blog posts, videos, infographics, and eBooks that resonate with your target market and demonstrate your expertise.

Search Engine Optimization (SEO)

Optimize your online content for search engines to improve your visibility in search results. Incorporate relevant keywords, optimize meta tags, and ensure fast loading times to enhance your SEO efforts.

Social Media Engagement

Leverage social media platforms to connect with your audience. Choose platforms that align with your target demographic and industry. Regularly share engaging content, interact with followers, and build a community.

Email Marketing Campaigns

Develop targeted email marketing campaigns to nurture relationships with your audience. Provide valuable content, exclusive offers, and personalized recommendations to keep your subscribers engaged.

Pay-Per-Click (PPC) Advertising

Utilize PPC advertising to promote your products or services on platforms like Google Ads or social media networks. Develop strategic campaigns that target specific keywords and demographics.

Influencer Collaborations

Partner with influencers or industry experts who align with your brand. Influencer collaborations can help you reach new audiences and establish credibility in your niche.

Online Reputation Management

Monitor and manage your online reputation through customer reviews, ratings, and feedback. Respond to reviews promptly and address any concerns to maintain a positive image.

Analytics and Data Insights

Utilize analytics tools to track the performance of your online efforts. Analyze metrics such as website traffic, social media engagement, and conversion rates. Use data insights to refine your strategies.

Continuous Improvement

Building an online presence is an ongoing endeavor. Regularly assess your strategies, gather feedback from your audience, and adapt to changing trends and technologies.

Building a strong online presence is not just about creating a website; it's about creating a digital ecosystem that resonates with your audience. As you delve into this chapter, remember that your online presence is a canvas for creativity and connection. Your mastery of this art empowers you to create a symphony of engagement, authenticity, and growth. Just as an artist carefully selects each brushstroke to convey a message, so too must you craft your online presence to tell the story of your brand, captivating and resonating with your audience in the ever-evolving digital landscape.

Creating a Professional Business Website

In the digital realm of business, a professional website serves as your virtual storefront, inviting visitors to explore your offerings and learn about your brand. This chapter delves into the art of creating a professional business website – a strategic pursuit that involves designing an intuitive user experience, optimizing for search engines, and crafting compelling content that resonates with your target audience. Just as an architect designs a functional and visually captivating building, so too must you design your website to captivate and engage online visitors.

Strategic Planning

Begin by outlining the goals and objectives of your website. Determine what you want to achieve – whether it's generating leads, selling products, or providing information. A clear plan guides the development process.

User-Centered Design

Design your website with the user in mind. Create an intuitive and user-friendly interface that guides visitors through the content. Consider user navigation, easy access to information, and responsive design for mobile devices.

Branding and Visual Identity

Incorporate your brand's visual identity into the website design. Use consistent colors, fonts, and imagery that align with your offline branding. A cohesive visual identity reinforces brand recognition.

Content Strategy

Develop a content strategy that speaks to your target audience's needs and interests. Craft compelling copy, engaging images, and multimedia content that effectively communicates your message and value proposition.

Clear Call-to-Action (CTA)

Strategically place clear and compelling CTAs throughout your website. These prompts encourage visitors to take desired actions, whether it's signing up for a newsletter, making a purchase, or requesting more information.

Search Engine Optimization (SEO)

Optimize your website's content and structure for search engines. Incorporate relevant keywords, meta tags, and descriptions to improve your visibility in search engine results.

Quality Imagery and Multimedia

Use high-quality images and multimedia elements to enhance the visual appeal of your website. Visual content should complement your written content and create an immersive experience for visitors.

Fast Loading Times

Ensure that your website loads quickly across devices and browsers. Slow-loading websites can lead to higher bounce rates and lower user satisfaction.

Contact Information and Accessibility

Display clear contact information, including phone numbers, email addresses, and physical addresses. Additionally, ensure that your website is accessible to users with disabilities, in compliance with accessibility guidelines.

Testimonials and Social Proof

Incorporate testimonials, reviews, and case studies that highlight the positive experiences of your customers. Social proof builds trust and credibility.

Analytics and Tracking

Integrate analytics tools to track user behavior on your website. Analyze metrics such as page views, click-through rates, and conversion rates to assess the effectiveness of your website's performance.

Continuous Improvement

Regularly review and update your website to ensure it remains current, relevant, and aligned with your business goals. Incorporate feedback from users to make iterative improvements.

Creating a professional business website is not just about design; it's about creating a digital gateway to your brand. As you immerse yourself in this chapter, remember that your website is a canvas for your business's online presence. Your mastery of this art empowers you to create a symphony of functionality, aesthetics, and engagement. Just as an architect designs a space for functionality and beauty, so too must you design your website to provide a seamless and visually appealing experience, inviting visitors to explore your brand and offerings in the digital world.

Leveraging Social Media for Brand Building

In the dynamic landscape of business, social media serves as a powerful tool for building your brand's presence, connecting with your audience, and fostering meaningful relationships. This chapter delves into the art of leveraging social media for brand building – a strategic pursuit that involves crafting a consistent brand image, engaging with followers, and using platforms to tell your brand's story. Just as a storyteller weaves tales that captivate an audience, so too must you use social media to tell the compelling story of your brand.

Platform Selection

Choose social media platforms that align with your target audience and brand identity. Whether it's Facebook, Instagram, Twitter, LinkedIn, or others, select platforms where your audience is most active.

Consistent Branding

Maintain consistent branding across all social media profiles. Use the same profile picture, cover photo, and brand colors to create a unified and recognizable brand presence.

Engaging Content

Craft content that resonates with your audience. Share informative, entertaining, and valuable content that aligns with your brand's values and interests. Mix up your content formats, including images, videos, infographics, and more.

Storytelling

Use social media to tell your brand's story. Share the journey, milestones, and behind-the-scenes moments that make your brand unique. Authentic storytelling builds emotional connections with your audience.

Interactive Engagement

Engage with your audience by responding to comments, messages, and mentions. Create polls, ask questions, and encourage discussions to foster meaningful interactions with followers.

Hashtags and Trends

Incorporate relevant hashtags to increase the visibility of your content. Stay updated on trending topics and participate in relevant conversations to expand your reach and relevance.

Visual Aesthetics

Maintain a visually appealing feed by curating images and content that align with your brand's visual identity. A cohesive aesthetic enhances your brand's overall appeal on social media.

Influencer Partnerships

Collaborate with influencers or industry experts to reach new audiences. Influencer partnerships can introduce your brand to a broader follower base and lend credibility to your products or services.

User-Generated Content

Encourage customers to create and share content related to your brand. Repost user-generated content to showcase customer loyalty and authenticity.

Analytics and Insights

Use social media analytics tools to track the performance of your posts and campaigns. Analyze metrics such as engagement rates, reach, and click-through rates to measure your impact.

Adaptation and Experimentation

Stay agile by adapting to changes in algorithms and user behaviors. Experiment with different content strategies and formats to discover what resonates most with your audience.

Leveraging social media for brand building is not just about posting; it's about building a community and fostering connections. As you delve into this chapter, remember that social media is a stage where your brand comes to life. Your mastery of this art empowers you to create a symphony of engagement, storytelling, and authenticity. Just as a storyteller captivates an audience with their words, so too must you captivate your online audience with content that resonates, engages, and reflects the unique essence of your brand.

Engaging with Customers Online

In the interconnected world of business, engaging with customers online is the bridge that forges lasting relationships and cultivates loyalty. This chapter delves into the art of engaging with customers online – a strategic pursuit that involves active communication, attentive listening, and providing exceptional customer experiences across digital channels. Just as a host ensures the comfort and enjoyment of their guests, so too must you create an inviting and enriching digital environment for your customers.

Responsive Communication

Respond promptly to customer inquiries, comments, and messages across digital platforms. Swift responses show that you value their time and are dedicated to addressing their needs.

Personalized Interactions

Tailor your interactions to each customer's preferences and needs. Use customer data to provide personalized recommendations, solutions, and offers that resonate with their interests.

Active Social Listening

Monitor social media and online platforms for mentions of your brand. Engage in conversations related to your industry, products, or services to demonstrate your expertise and foster meaningful connections.

Customer Feedback

Encourage customers to share their feedback and opinions. Actively seek out feedback through surveys, polls, and reviews to understand their experiences and make improvements.

Online Communities

Create or participate in online communities and forums related to your industry or niche. Engage in discussions, answer questions, and offer valuable insights to establish yourself as an authoritative figure.

Transparency and Authenticity

Be transparent about your brand's values, practices, and products. Authenticity builds trust and resonates with customers who appreciate honest interactions.

User-Generated Content

Acknowledge and celebrate user-generated content shared by customers. Repost their content on your social media channels to show appreciation and reinforce a sense of community.

Surprise and Delight

Occasionally surprise customers with unexpected rewards, discounts, or personalized messages. These gestures foster positive sentiment and enhance the customer experience.

Timely Issue Resolution

Address customer concerns and issues promptly. Offer solutions and rectify any problems to showcase your commitment to customer satisfaction.

Engagement Campaigns

Launch engagement campaigns that encourage customers to share their experiences or participate in challenges. These campaigns drive interaction and create a sense of involvement.

Continuous Improvement

Use customer interactions as a source of insights for improving your products, services, and processes. Listening to your customers helps you align your business with their needs.

Engaging with customers online is not just about interactions; it's about nurturing relationships. As you immerse yourself in this chapter, remember that online engagement is a dialogue that spans beyond transactions. Your mastery of this art empowers you to create a symphony of connection, empathy, and loyalty. Just as a gracious host ensures their guests feel valued and cared for, so too must you ensure that every online customer interaction reflects your commitment to their satisfaction and enjoyment, fostering relationships that resonate and endure.

Expanding Your Customer Base

In the ever-evolving landscape of business, expanding your customer base is the pursuit that propels your brand toward new growth horizons. This chapter delves into the art of expanding your customer base – a strategic endeavor that involves reaching new markets, attracting diverse demographics, and nurturing relationships with potential customers. Just as an explorer charts uncharted territories, so too must you venture into new realms to cultivate a broader audience for your brand.

Market Research and Segmentation

Conduct thorough market research to identify untapped segments and potential customer groups. Segment your target market based on demographics, behaviors, and preferences.

Customer Profiling

Create detailed customer profiles for each target segment. Understand their pain points, needs, desires, and buying behaviors. This insight guides your marketing and messaging strategies.

Tailored Marketing Strategies

Develop marketing strategies tailored to each target segment. Craft messages and campaigns that resonate with their specific interests and motivations.

Digital Marketing Channels

Leverage digital marketing channels such as social media, content marketing, SEO, and paid advertising to reach a wider audience. Utilize platforms where your target demographics are most active.

Geographic Expansion

Consider expanding your operations to new geographic areas. Research and adapt to local market nuances, preferences, and cultural factors.

Partnerships and Alliances

Form partnerships with complementary businesses to access their customer base. Collaborations can introduce your brand to a broader audience.

Referral and Affiliate Programs

Implement referral programs that incentivize your current customers to refer new customers. Affiliate programs can also help you tap into other businesses' networks.

Special Offers and Promotions

Attract new customers with special offers, discounts, or limited-time promotions. These incentives encourage potential customers to try your products or services.

Content Marketing

Create valuable and educational content that addresses your target audience's needs. Content marketing establishes your brand as an authoritative source and attracts new customers.

Networking and Events

Participate in industry events, trade shows, and networking opportunities to connect with potential customers and industry professionals.

Influencer Collaborations

Collaborate with influencers who resonate with your target audience. Influencers can introduce your brand to their followers and build trust on your behalf.

Feedback and Adaptation

Use customer feedback and data insights to adapt your strategies. Continuously refine your approach based on customer responses and market trends.

Expanding your customer base is not just about reaching more people; it's about forging connections with diverse audiences. As you delve into this chapter, remember that expansion is a journey that requires strategic navigation. Your mastery of this art empowers you to create a symphony of exploration, innovation, and connection. Just as an explorer embraces new horizons, so too must you embrace new possibilities and audiences, enriching your brand's landscape with diversity and growth.

Building Customer Loyalty Programs

In the intricate realm of business, customer loyalty is the foundation upon which lasting relationships are built. This chapter delves into the art of creating customer loyalty programs – a strategic pursuit that involves rewarding and engaging your loyal customers to foster repeat business, advocacy, and brand affinity. Just as a gardener tends to their plants, so too must you nurture your customer relationships to cultivate a loyal and devoted audience for your brand.

Understanding Customer Loyalty

Begin by understanding the importance of customer loyalty. Loyal customers not only bring repeat business but also serve as brand advocates who spread positive word-of-mouth.

Segmenting Your Customer Base

Segment your customer base to tailor loyalty programs to different customer groups. Consider factors such as purchase frequency, spending habits, and demographics.

Reward Structure

Design a reward structure that incentivizes customers to engage with your loyalty program. Offer rewards such as discounts, exclusive offers, free products, or access to special events.

Points-Based Systems

Implement a points-based system where customers earn points for each purchase. Accumulated points can be redeemed for rewards, encouraging repeat purchases.

Tiered Loyalty Programs

Create tiered loyalty programs that offer escalating rewards as customers reach higher levels of engagement or spending. This structure motivates customers to achieve higher tiers.

Personalization

Personalize loyalty program interactions based on customer preferences and behaviors. Send personalized offers and recommendations that resonate with individual customers.

Exclusive Content and Experiences

Provide loyal customers with exclusive content, sneak peeks, or access to events that are not available to the general public. These perks make them feel valued and appreciated.

Communication Strategies

Communicate regularly with loyalty program members. Keep them informed about their rewards balance, upcoming promotions, and special events.

User-Friendly Mobile App or Platform

If feasible, create a user-friendly mobile app or online platform for your loyalty program. This allows customers to easily track their rewards, earn points, and redeem rewards.

Social Media Engagement

Engage with loyalty program members on social media platforms. Encourage them to share their experiences and rewards with their followers, extending your program's reach.

Referral Rewards

Incorporate referral rewards into your loyalty program. Encourage loyal customers to refer friends and family in exchange for additional rewards.

Feedback and Adaptation

Gather feedback from loyalty program members and adapt the program based on their suggestions. Demonstrating responsiveness to their needs fosters a sense of ownership.

Building customer loyalty programs is not just about rewards; it's about building relationships. As you immerse yourself in this chapter, remember that loyalty programs are a testament to your commitment to customer satisfaction. Your mastery of this art empowers you to create a symphony of appreciation, engagement, and advocacy. Just as a gardener nurtures their plants to flourish, so too must you nurture your customer relationships, cultivating a garden of devoted brand advocates who continually enrich your business's ecosystem.

Implementing Referral and Word-of-Mouth Strategies

In the interconnected landscape of business, harnessing the power of referrals and word-of-mouth can amplify your brand's reach and credibility. This chapter delves into the art of implementing referral and word-of-mouth strategies – a strategic pursuit that involves encouraging satisfied customers to spread the word about your offerings, driving organic growth and fostering trust. Just as a ripple in a pond expands outward, so too can positive experiences create waves of influence that resonate far and wide.

Recognizing the Impact

Begin by understanding the profound impact of referrals and word-of-mouth. Recommendations from friends, family, or colleagues carry a high level of trust and influence over purchasing decisions.

Customer-Centric Experiences

Deliver exceptional customer experiences that leave a positive impression. Satisfied customers are more likely to share their experiences with others.

Referral Programs

Implement a formal referral program that rewards customers for referring new customers. Offer incentives such as discounts, free products, or exclusive perks to both the referrer and the referred.

Clear Communication

Clearly communicate your referral program to existing customers. Make it easy for them to understand how the program works and how they can participate.

Social Sharing and Sharing Buttons

Include social sharing buttons on your website and marketing materials. Encourage customers to share their positive experiences with their social networks.

Email Campaigns

Send targeted email campaigns to your customer base, inviting them to refer friends or family members. Provide them with clear instructions on how to participate.

Personalized Recommendations

Use data and insights to provide personalized recommendations to customers. Show them products or services that align with their preferences, increasing the likelihood of referrals.

Social Proof

Leverage user-generated content, testimonials, and reviews to showcase the positive experiences of your customers. Social proof reinforces the credibility of your offerings.

Influencer Collaborations

Collaborate with influencers or brand advocates who resonate with your target audience. Their endorsement can carry significant weight and drive word-of-mouth referrals.

Engagement and Interactions

Engage with your customers on social media and other online platforms. Respond to their comments, questions, and feedback to foster a sense of connection.

Measurement and Optimization

Track the success of your referral and word-of-mouth strategies. Monitor metrics such as referral rates, social media engagement, and website traffic to assess their impact.

Implementing referral and word-of-mouth strategies is not just about spreading the word; it's about nurturing a community of brand advocates. As you delve into this chapter, remember that positive experiences have the potential to ripple outward, creating a network of trust and influence. Your mastery of this art empowers you to create a symphony of authenticity, connection, and growth. Just as a whisper can spread across a room, so too can positive recommendations and experiences reverberate through networks, amplifying your brand's impact and forging connections that stand the test of time.

Exploring New Geographical Markets

In the ever-expanding realm of business, exploring new geographical markets is the journey that opens doors to fresh opportunities and growth. This chapter delves into the art of venturing into new markets – a strategic pursuit that involves understanding diverse cultures, adapting to local preferences, and establishing your brand presence in uncharted territories. Just as an explorer charts new lands, so too must you embark on a journey of discovery to connect with audiences in different corners of the world.

Market Research and Analysis

Begin by conducting thorough market research of the new geographical markets you're considering. Understand the local consumer behavior, preferences, competition, and cultural nuances.

Target Audience Segmentation

Segment your target audience within the new market based on demographics, psychographics, and other relevant factors. Tailor your strategies to resonate with their needs and values.

Cultural Sensitivity

Respect and adapt to the cultural norms and values of the new market. Consider language, customs, and traditions to avoid misunderstandings and build positive relationships.

Local Partnerships

Establish partnerships with local businesses or individuals who understand the market dynamics. Their insights and connections can provide valuable guidance as you navigate the new market.

Adapting Products and Services

Adapt your products or services to meet the specific needs and preferences of the new market. Customize offerings to align with local tastes and requirements.

Market Entry Strategies

Choose a market entry strategy that suits the new market. This could include options such as exporting, franchising, licensing, joint ventures, or direct investment.

Distribution Channels

Identify appropriate distribution channels for reaching your target audience. Consider local retailers, distributors, online platforms, or other methods that align with the market's buying habits.

Localized Marketing Campaigns

Develop marketing campaigns that resonate with the local audience. Use culturally relevant imagery, messaging, and channels to establish an emotional connection.

Regulatory and Legal Considerations

Understand and comply with local regulations, taxes, and legal requirements. Work with legal experts to navigate any complexities associated with entering the new market.

Pricing Strategies

Set pricing strategies that consider local purchasing power, competition, and economic factors. Ensure that your pricing aligns with market expectations.

Test and Iterate

Start with a small-scale test to assess the viability of the new market. Gather feedback, monitor performance, and be prepared to iterate your strategies based on the results.

Exploring new geographical markets is not just about expansion; it's about building bridges across cultures and boundaries. As you delve into this chapter, remember that every new market holds a unique tapestry of opportunities and challenges. Your mastery of this art empowers you to create a symphony of adaptability, cultural awareness, and growth. Just as an explorer embraces the unknown with curiosity and courage, so too must you embark on the journey of market exploration, expanding your brand's horizons and weaving connections that transcend geographical boundaries.

Hiring and Developing a Winning Team

In the intricate world of business, a winning team is the backbone that propels your company toward success. This chapter delves into the art of hiring and developing a winning team – a strategic pursuit that involves identifying top talent, fostering a culture of collaboration, and nurturing the skills and potential of your employees. Just as a conductor orchestrates a harmonious ensemble, so too must you assemble and nurture a team that creates a symphony of achievement and growth.

Strategic Workforce Planning

Begin by outlining your business's goals and identifying the skills and roles needed to achieve them. Develop a strategic workforce plan that aligns with your company's vision.

Effective Recruitment

Craft job descriptions that clearly outline responsibilities, qualifications, and expectations. Utilize diverse recruitment channels to attract a broad pool of qualified candidates.

Cultural Fit

Assess candidates for cultural fit in addition to skills and experience. A cohesive team thrives when members share common values, work ethic, and a collaborative mindset.

Behavioral Interviews

Conduct behavioral interviews that delve into candidates' past experiences and actions. This helps gauge their problem-solving abilities, communication skills, and how they handle challenges.

Onboarding Excellence

Provide a comprehensive onboarding process that familiarizes new employees with your company's culture, values, and expectations. A strong onboarding experience sets the tone for their journey.

Skill Development

Offer ongoing training and professional development opportunities for your team members. Invest in their growth to enhance their skills, boost morale, and increase their overall contribution.

Performance Management

Implement a performance management system that provides regular feedback and evaluations. Recognize achievements and address areas for improvement to facilitate continuous growth.

Effective Communication

Promote open and transparent communication within the team. Encourage regular check-ins, team meetings, and opportunities for sharing ideas and feedback.

Empowerment and Autonomy

Empower your team members by delegating responsibilities and granting them autonomy to make decisions within their roles. Trust and autonomy foster a sense of ownership.

Recognition and Rewards

Acknowledge and reward your team's achievements and contributions. A culture of recognition boosts morale, encourages continued dedication, and fosters a positive work environment.

Conflict Resolution

Develop effective conflict resolution strategies to address disputes or disagreements within the team. Promote a respectful and inclusive atmosphere for addressing challenges.

Leadership Development

Identify and nurture leadership potential within your team. Offer mentorship and growth opportunities to employees who show leadership qualities.

Hiring and developing a winning team is not just about assembling talent; it's about cultivating a culture of collaboration and growth. As you immerse yourself in this chapter, remember that a winning team is a harmonious symphony of diverse talents working toward a shared vision. Your mastery of this art empowers you to create an orchestra of achievement, synergy, and progress. Just as a conductor guides each musician to create beautiful music, so too must you guide your team members to work in harmony, achieving remarkable feats that resonate throughout your business's journey toward success.

Identifying Key Roles for Growth

In the strategic landscape of business, identifying key roles for growth is the compass that directs your company's expansion efforts. This chapter delves into the art of recognizing pivotal roles that drive progress and innovation – a pursuit that involves understanding your business's evolving needs, pinpointing areas that require expertise, and assembling a team that strategically aligns with your growth objectives. Just as a captain selects a skilled crew to navigate uncharted waters, so too must you assemble a team that propels your business toward new horizons.

Strategic Business Analysis

Begin by conducting a comprehensive analysis of your business's growth goals and objectives. Identify areas where additional talent is needed to support your expansion plans.

Visionary Leadership

Appoint visionary leaders who can guide your company through growth. These leaders should possess strategic thinking, adaptability, and the ability to inspire and align teams.

Sales and Business Development

Recruit professionals who excel in sales and business development. These individuals play a crucial role in expanding your customer base, building relationships, and driving revenue growth.

Marketing and Branding

Bring in experts in marketing and branding to elevate your business's visibility and appeal. A strong marketing team can effectively communicate your value proposition and attract new customers.

Product Development and Innovation

Identify individuals who are skilled in product development and innovation. These roles are essential for creating new offerings that meet market demands and differentiate your business.

Operations and Efficiency

Hire individuals who specialize in operations and process optimization. They can streamline internal workflows, improve efficiency, and ensure smooth scaling without compromising quality.

Technology and IT

Recruit IT professionals who can support your technological infrastructure and digital initiatives. As technology evolves, having a strong IT team is critical for maintaining competitiveness.

Finance and Strategy

Appoint professionals with expertise in finance and strategic planning. They can provide valuable insights on budgeting, financial management, and investment decisions.

Customer Experience and Support

Bring in individuals who are dedicated to enhancing customer experience. A strong customer support team can foster loyalty and drive word-of-mouth referrals.

Project Management

Identify individuals skilled in project management who can oversee the execution of growth initiatives. Effective project management ensures that plans are executed on time and within budget.

Cross-Functional Collaboration

Encourage cross-functional collaboration among key roles. A cohesive team that works collaboratively can drive alignment and synergy across various business functions.

Continuous Evaluation and Adaptation

Regularly evaluate the performance and effectiveness of key roles. Be prepared to adapt your team structure as your business's needs evolve.

Identifying key roles for growth is not just about filling positions; it's about strategically assembling a team that drives your business forward. As you delve into this chapter, remember that each role contributes to the larger symphony of your business's success. Your mastery of this art empowers you to create a symphony of expertise, collaboration, and progress. Just as a conductor selects musicians to harmonize their talents, so too must you orchestrate a team that collaboratively works together, achieving remarkable results that resonate with your business's journey toward growth and prosperity.

Attracting and Retaining Top Talent

In the dynamic landscape of business, attracting and retaining top talent is the foundation upon which your company's success is built. This chapter delves into the art of creating a workplace that draws in exceptional individuals, fosters their growth, and ensures their long-term commitment – a strategic pursuit that involves showcasing your company's value proposition, cultivating a supportive environment, and providing opportunities for advancement. Just as a magnet pulls in precious metals, so too must you create a workplace that attracts and retains the brightest minds.

Crafting a Compelling Employer Brand

Begin by defining and communicating your company's unique employer brand. Highlight the benefits, values, and culture that make your workplace an appealing destination for top talent.

Competitive Compensation and Benefits

Offer competitive compensation packages that reflect the value of the skills and contributions you seek. Provide comprehensive benefits that cater to employees' well-being and work-life balance.

Professional Growth Opportunities

Create a clear path for professional growth and advancement within your organization. Showcase opportunities for skill development, promotions, and leadership roles.

Inclusive and Diverse Culture

Cultivate an inclusive and diverse workplace where all employees feel valued and respected. Diversity enhances creativity and innovation, contributing to a thriving work environment.

Flexible Work Arrangements

Offer flexible work arrangements, such as remote work options or flexible hours. This accommodates diverse lifestyles and promotes work-life balance.

Meaningful Work

Emphasize the meaningful impact of the work employees will contribute to. Show how their efforts align with the company's mission and goals.

Recognition and Rewards

Implement a recognition program that acknowledges and celebrates employees' achievements. Regularly reward exceptional performance to foster motivation and a sense of accomplishment.

Supportive Leadership

Promote supportive leadership that listens to employees, provides guidance, and empowers them to make decisions.

Approachable leadership builds trust and loyalty.

Workplace Wellness Programs

Invest in workplace wellness programs that promote physical, mental, and emotional well-being. These initiatives demonstrate your commitment to employees' health.

Feedback and Development

Provide consistent feedback to employees on their performance and growth. Offer opportunities for skill development and address areas for improvement.

Workplace Flexibility

Create a work environment that accommodates individual preferences and needs. Offer options for remote work, flexible hours, and other arrangements.

Retention Strategies

Implement retention strategies such as mentorship programs, ongoing learning opportunities, and career planning to encourage employees to stay and grow within your organization.

Attracting and retaining top talent is not just about recruitment; it's about building a community of motivated and engaged individuals. As you immerse yourself in this chapter, remember that your workplace is a canvas for professional growth and fulfillment. Your mastery of this art empowers you to create a symphony of opportunity, support, and appreciation. Just as a magnet draws in precious materials, so too must you create a workplace that attracts and retains exceptional talent, fostering a culture where individuals flourish and contribute their best to your business's journey toward success.

Providing Training and Growth Opportunities

In the evolving landscape of business, providing training and growth opportunities is the conduit through which your employees develop their skills, contribute meaningfully, and propel your company forward. This chapter delves into the art of fostering a culture of continuous learning and development – a strategic pursuit that involves offering structured training, mentorship, and avenues for skill enhancement. Just as a gardener nurtures plants to flourish, so too must you nurture your employees to bloom with knowledge and capability.

Assessing Skills and Needs

Begin by assessing the skills and competencies of your employees. Identify areas where training and development can enhance their performance and contribute to organizational goals.

Structured Training Programs

Design structured training programs that address specific skill gaps and align with business objectives. These programs can range from onboarding sessions to ongoing professional development.

Mentorship and Coaching

Implement mentorship and coaching programs that pair experienced employees with those seeking to learn and grow.

Mentors provide guidance, insights, and a safe space for exploration.

Cross-Functional Exposure

Offer opportunities for employees to work on projects outside their usual scope. Exposure to different areas of the business fosters a broader skillset and cross-functional understanding.

Skill Enhancement Workshops

Host workshops, seminars, and webinars that focus on specific skills relevant to your industry. These events provide targeted learning experiences and networking opportunities.

Leadership Development

Create leadership development programs to identify and nurture potential leaders within your organization. Leadership training empowers employees to take on more responsibility.

Online Learning Platforms

Provide access to online learning platforms that offer a wide range of courses and resources. This allows employees to pursue self-directed learning at their own pace.

Feedback and Performance Reviews

Incorporate training discussions into regular performance reviews. Use these conversations to set development goals and identify training needs.

Encourage Curiosity

Foster a culture of curiosity and continuous learning. Encourage employees to ask questions, seek out new challenges, and explore innovative solutions.

Recognition and Reward for Learning

Recognize and reward employees who actively engage in learning and skill enhancement. Acknowledging their efforts reinforces the value of personal and professional growth.

Alignment with Career Goals

Tailor training and growth opportunities to align with employees' career aspirations. This shows that you are invested in their long-term success.

Providing training and growth opportunities is not just about skill-building; it's about cultivating a culture of empowerment and development. As you delve into this chapter, remember that your workplace is a canvas for continuous improvement and evolution. Your mastery of this art empowers you to create a symphony of growth, expertise, and achievement. Just as a gardener nurtures plants to flourish, so too must you nurture your employees' potential, allowing them to thrive and contribute their best to your business's journey toward excellence.

Measuring and Tracking Growth

In the dynamic world of business, measuring and tracking growth is the compass that guides your company's progress and informs strategic decisions. This chapter delves into the art of quantifying and assessing your business's expansion – a strategic pursuit that involves analyzing key performance indicators, collecting data-driven insights, and adapting your strategies based on real-time feedback. Just as a navigator uses tools to chart a course, so too must you employ metrics to steer your business toward sustainable growth.

Defining Key Performance Indicators (KPIs)

Begin by identifying the KPIs that align with your business's goals. These indicators could encompass financial metrics, customer acquisition, retention rates, market share, or other relevant measures.

SMART Goal Setting

Set Specific, Measurable, Achievable, Relevant, and Time-bound (SMART) goals that provide clear benchmarks for growth. SMART goals keep your team aligned and focused on measurable outcomes.

Regular Data Collection

Implement systems for collecting accurate and relevant data related to your chosen

KPIs. Use both qualitative and quantitative data sources to gain a comprehensive view.

Data Analysis

Analyze the collected data to gain insights into your business's performance trends and areas for improvement. Data analysis helps you identify strengths and weaknesses.

Comparative Analysis

Benchmark your business's performance against industry standards and competitors. Comparative analysis provides context and reveals opportunities for growth.

Performance Dashboards

Create performance dashboards that visually represent your KPIs and track progress over time. Dashboards provide a quick snapshot of your business's growth trajectory.

Trend Identification

Identify growth trends by observing patterns in your data over different time periods. This enables you to project future growth and make informed decisions.

Regular Reporting

Provide regular reports to your team and stakeholders that highlight your business's growth performance. Transparent reporting fosters accountability and informed decision-making.

Feedback Loops

Establish feedback loops that encourage continuous improvement. Use data insights to adjust strategies, allocate resources, and pivot when necessary.

Customer Feedback and Satisfaction

Incorporate customer feedback and satisfaction metrics into your growth tracking. Happy customers are often indicative of successful growth strategies.

Adapting Strategies

Based on the insights gained from data analysis, be prepared to adapt your strategies to optimize growth. Agility and flexibility are crucial for staying competitive.

Measuring and tracking growth is not just about numbers; it's about informed decision-making and strategic refinement. As you delve into this chapter, remember that data is your compass in the journey of growth. Your mastery of this art empowers you to create a symphony of insights, actions, and progress. Just as a navigator relies on instruments to steer a ship, so too must you rely on metrics to navigate your business toward sustainable growth, making informed choices that harmonize with your business's ongoing journey toward success.

Key Performance Indicators (KPIs) for Growth

In the strategic realm of business, Key Performance Indicators (KPIs) are the compass that guides your company's growth journey. This chapter delves into the art of identifying and utilizing KPIs – a strategic pursuit that involves selecting measurable metrics to monitor progress, assess success, and drive strategic decisions. Just as a navigator relies on constellations to chart a course, so too must you rely on KPIs to navigate your business toward its growth objectives.

Revenue Growth

Monitor the increase in your company's revenue over specific time periods. Revenue growth is a fundamental indicator of your business's overall health and expansion.

Customer Acquisition Cost (CAC)

Calculate the cost of acquiring a new customer, including marketing, sales, and operational expenses. A decreasing CAC indicates efficient customer acquisition strategies.

Customer Lifetime Value (CLTV)

Estimate the total value a customer brings to your business over their lifetime. CLTV helps you prioritize high-value customers and tailor retention efforts.

Gross Profit Margin

Calculate the percentage of revenue that remains after subtracting the cost of goods sold (COGS). A healthy gross profit margin indicates your ability to generate profits from sales.

Net Promoter Score (NPS)

Measure customer loyalty and satisfaction by assessing how likely customers are to recommend your business to others. A high NPS indicates strong customer advocacy.

Churn Rate

Track the rate at which customers discontinue using your products or services. A low churn rate suggests a higher level of customer retention and satisfaction.

Customer Retention Rate

Calculate the percentage of customers who continue doing business with you over time.

A high retention rate indicates strong customer relationships.

Conversion Rate

Measure the percentage of visitors who take a desired action, such as making a purchase or signing up for a newsletter. Conversion rate highlights the effectiveness of your marketing efforts.

Website Traffic and Engagement

Monitor the number of visitors to your website and their level of engagement. Website traffic and engagement reflect the effectiveness of your online presence.

Return on Investment (ROI)

Evaluate the return on investment for specific marketing campaigns or growth initiatives. Positive ROI indicates that your efforts are generating value.

Market Share

Assess your company's share of the total market sales within your industry. Increasing market share indicates your business's growth compared to competitors.

Employee Productivity and Satisfaction

Measure employee productivity, engagement, and satisfaction. Satisfied employees are more likely to contribute to your business's growth.

New Product/Service Adoption Rate

Track the rate at which customers adopt new offerings. High adoption rates indicate successful product launches and potential growth opportunities.

Key Performance Indicators (KPIs) for growth are not just numbers; they are the stars guiding your business toward success. As you delve into this chapter, remember that KPIs are your compass in the journey of growth. Your mastery of this art empowers you to create a symphony of insights, actions, and progress. Just as a navigator relies on constellations to guide a ship, so too must you rely on KPIs to navigate your business toward its strategic destination, making informed choices that resonate with your business's ongoing journey toward prosperity and achievement.

Monitoring and Analyzing Business Metrics

In the analytical landscape of business, monitoring and analyzing metrics is the compass that guides your strategic decisions and ensures your company's success. This chapter delves into the art of tracking and dissecting business metrics – a strategic pursuit that involves collecting data, interpreting trends, and extracting actionable insights to drive informed choices. Just as a detective scrutinizes evidence to solve a case, so too must you dissect metrics to uncover the story they tell about your business's performance.

Data Collection and Aggregation

Begin by setting up systems to collect relevant data from various sources, such as sales, marketing, finance, and operations. Aggregate data to create a comprehensive view.

Real-time Tracking

Implement tools and dashboards that allow you to track metrics in real time. Real-time tracking enables you to respond quickly to changes and trends.

Identify Key Metrics

Determine which metrics align with your business's goals and objectives. Focus on a core set of key metrics that provide actionable insights.

Establish Baselines

Create baseline measurements for each metric to establish a starting point. Baselines help you track growth and identify deviations from expected performance.

Periodic Analysis

Regularly analyze your metrics on a scheduled basis, such as weekly, monthly, or quarterly. Consistent analysis helps you identify trends and patterns.

Comparative Analysis

Benchmark your metrics against historical data, industry averages, or competitor performance. Comparative analysis provides context and identifies areas for improvement.

Data Visualization

Use data visualization tools to create charts, graphs, and visual representations of your metrics. Visualization enhances your understanding of trends and patterns.

Identify Correlations

Identify correlations between different metrics. Understanding how metrics influence one another can lead to insights for optimizing strategies.

Root Cause Analysis

When metrics deviate from expected values, perform root cause analysis to uncover the underlying factors. Addressing root causes can lead to improvements.

Predictive Analytics

Explore predictive analytics to forecast future performance based on historical data trends. Predictive insights help you make proactive decisions.

Continuous Improvement

Use metric analysis to inform continuous improvement initiatives. Make strategic adjustments based on insights to optimize your business's performance.

Effective Communication

Share metric insights and findings with your team and stakeholders. Effective communication fosters a data-driven decision-making culture.

Monitoring and analyzing business metrics is not just about numbers; it's about unraveling the story behind your business's performance. As you delve into this chapter, remember that metrics are the evidence that inform your strategic choices. Your mastery of this art empowers you to create a symphony of insights, actions, and progress. Just as a detective uncovers clues to solve a mystery, so too must you analyze metrics to uncover insights that guide your business toward success, piecing together the puzzle of growth and achievement.

Adjusting Strategies Based on Data Insights

In the dynamic realm of business, adjusting strategies based on data insights is the compass that guides your company's evolution and resilience. This chapter delves into the art of translating data-driven insights into actionable strategies – a strategic pursuit that involves interpreting trends, identifying opportunities, and making informed adjustments to optimize your business's trajectory. Just as a pilot adjusts a flight path based on weather data, so too must you steer your business with agility and precision using the insights provided by data.

Interpreting Data Trends

Begin by closely examining the trends and patterns within your collected data. Identify anomalies, shifts, and correlations that can inform your decision-making.

Alignment with Goals

Assess how current strategies align with your business's overarching goals and objectives. Ensure that any adjustments support your mission and vision.

Identify Opportunities

Use data insights to uncover untapped opportunities or emerging trends. Identify areas where your business can pivot or expand to capitalize on market shifts.

Prioritizing Insights

Determine which data insights are most impactful and relevant to your immediate business needs. Focus on insights that can drive meaningful changes.

Testing Hypotheses

Formulate hypotheses based on data observations and test them through controlled experiments or pilot programs. This empirical approach helps validate insights.

Adapting Marketing Strategies

Utilize data insights to refine your marketing strategies. Adjust messaging, targeting, and channels based on customer behavior and preferences.

Optimizing Operations

Analyze operational data to identify inefficiencies and bottlenecks. Adjust workflows, processes, and resource allocation to enhance efficiency.

Personalization and Customer Experience

Leverage data insights to personalize customer experiences. Tailor offerings and interactions based on individual preferences and behaviors.

Innovating Products/Services

Incorporate data feedback into product or service innovation. Launch enhancements or new offerings that directly address customer needs and pain points.

Competitor Analysis

Use data to analyze your competitors' performance and market positioning. Adjust your strategies to differentiate and stay ahead in the competitive landscape.

Flexibility and Agility

Embrace a culture of flexibility and agility that allows for rapid strategy adjustments. Being adaptable positions your business to respond to changing circumstances.

Measuring Impact

After making strategy adjustments, monitor the impact on relevant metrics. Compare performance before and after changes to assess effectiveness.

Adjusting strategies based on data insights is not just about numbers; it's about staying responsive and relevant in a rapidly changing environment. As you delve into this chapter, remember that data insights are your compass for strategic evolution. Your mastery of this art empowers you to create a symphony of adaptability, innovation, and progress. Just as a pilot adjusts course to navigate through turbulence, so too must you adjust strategies to navigate your business through dynamic landscapes, making informed choices that orchestrate your business's journey toward resilience and success.

Overcoming Challenges and Risks

In the intricate terrain of business, overcoming challenges and risks is the armor that fortifies your company's resilience and growth. This chapter delves into the art of addressing obstacles and navigating risks – a strategic pursuit that involves identifying potential pitfalls, developing mitigation strategies, and embracing a proactive mindset. Just as a mountaineer conquers treacherous peaks, so too must you ascend challenges and risks with determination and strategic finesse.

Risk Identification and Assessment

Begin by identifying potential risks and challenges that your business may encounter. Assess their potential impact on various aspects of your operations.

Risk Mitigation Strategies

Develop comprehensive strategies to mitigate identified risks. These strategies may include contingency plans, diversification, insurance, and alternative approaches.

Scenario Planning

Anticipate different scenarios that could arise due to challenges or risks. Develop plans for each scenario to ensure preparedness and agility.

Data-Driven Decision-Making

Use data and insights to inform your decisions related to challenges and risks.

Analyze trends and historical patterns to guide your strategies.

Crisis Management

Establish a crisis management plan that outlines roles, responsibilities, and protocols in the event of unexpected challenges or crises.

Adaptable Leadership

Foster adaptable leadership that can pivot and make swift decisions in response to challenges. Encourage a culture of agility and innovative problem-solving.

Communication Strategies

Develop effective communication strategies to address challenges transparently with stakeholders. Open communication builds trust and credibility.

Team Empowerment

Empower your team to contribute solutions and ideas for overcoming challenges. Collective intelligence often leads to creative problem-solving.

Continuous Improvement

Embrace a mindset of continuous improvement, using challenges as opportunities to learn and grow. Reflect on lessons learned and apply them to future strategies.

Financial Resilience

Maintain a solid financial foundation to buffer against unexpected challenges. Build reserves and diversify revenue streams to increase financial resilience.

Collaborative Partnerships

Cultivate partnerships with other businesses or organizations that can provide support during challenging times. Collaboration can enhance resources and expertise.

Adaptive Innovation

Harness innovation to adapt your business model, products, or services in response to challenges. Innovative solutions often lead to breakthroughs.

Overcoming challenges and risks is not just about survival; it's about building strength and resilience. As you immerse yourself in this chapter, remember that challenges are opportunities for growth. Your mastery of this art empowers you to create a symphony of perseverance, strategy, and progress. Just as a mountaineer conquers treacherous peaks with unwavering determination, so too must you navigate challenges and risks with a steadfast spirit, ensuring that your business's journey continues upward toward success and triumph.

Anticipating and Addressing Growing Pains

In the expansive landscape of business, anticipating and addressing growing pains is the compass that steers your company through the complexities of expansion. This chapter delves into the art of recognizing and proactively managing the challenges that arise as your business scales – a strategic pursuit that involves identifying potential bottlenecks, optimizing processes, and fostering a culture of adaptability. Just as a seasoned navigator anticipates rough waters, so too must you prepare for and navigate the challenges that come with growth.

Scalability Assessment

Begin by assessing your business's current processes, resources, and infrastructure to determine their scalability as demand increases.

Process Optimization

Streamline and optimize your business processes to accommodate higher volumes without compromising efficiency. Identify bottlenecks and inefficiencies and implement improvements.

Resource Allocation

Allocate resources effectively to ensure that your business can handle increased demands. This includes manpower, technology, and financial resources.

Technology Upgrades

Invest in technology upgrades that support growth and increase operational efficiency. Modern systems can automate tasks and improve overall performance.

Employee Development

Foster a culture of continuous learning and development among your employees. Equip them with the skills they need to adapt to changing demands.

Clear Communication

Maintain clear communication channels within your organization to ensure that everyone is aligned with the company's growth objectives and challenges.

Adaptive Leadership

Lead with adaptability and flexibility. A leadership team that can pivot and adjust strategies as needed is crucial during periods of rapid growth.

Customer Experience

Prioritize maintaining a high level of customer experience even as your business expands. Satisfied customers remain loyal, helping sustain growth.

Supply Chain Optimization

Optimize your supply chain to ensure that you can meet increased demand while managing inventory levels, production, and distribution effectively.

Financial Planning

Plan and manage your finances strategically to accommodate increased costs associated with growth. Keep a close eye on cash flow and budgeting.

Cultural Preservation

As your business grows, preserve the core values and culture that defined your company from the start. A strong company culture can anchor your team during transitions.

Feedback and Adaptation

Gather feedback from employees, customers, and stakeholders to identify areas where adjustments are needed. Be willing to adapt based on feedback.

Anticipating and addressing growing pains is not just about overcoming obstacles; it's about thriving amidst change. As you delve into this chapter, remember that growth brings challenges that can be navigated with foresight and strategy. Your mastery of this art empowers you to create a symphony of adaptability, innovation, and progress. Just as a skilled navigator prepares for rough waters, so too must you navigate the waves of growth with resilience, steering your business toward new horizons of success and fulfillment.

Managing Financial and Operational Risks

In the dynamic landscape of business, managing financial and operational risks is the armor that safeguards your company's stability and growth. This chapter delves into the art of identifying, assessing, and mitigating risks that can impact your business's financial health and operational efficiency – a strategic pursuit that involves careful planning, contingency measures, and a proactive approach to safeguarding your business's resilience. Just as a fortress is fortified to withstand external threats, so too must you fortify your business against potential risks.

Risk Identification and Assessment

Begin by identifying potential financial and operational risks that your business may face. These could include market volatility, supply chain disruptions, regulatory changes, and more.

Quantitative Analysis

Conduct quantitative analysis to assess the potential impact of identified risks. Calculate potential financial losses and other consequences associated with each risk.

Risk Mitigation Strategies

Develop comprehensive risk mitigation strategies for each identified risk. These strategies may include risk transfer (insurance), risk avoidance, risk reduction, and risk acceptance.

Diversification

Diversify your revenue streams and customer base to reduce dependency on a single source. Diversification can help your business weather fluctuations in demand.

Emergency Fund

Maintain an emergency fund or reserve to cover unexpected financial setbacks. Having a cushion can help your business continue operations during challenging times.

Supply Chain Management

Assess and manage risks within your supply chain. Identify alternative suppliers and create contingency plans to address potential disruptions.

Scenario Planning

Create scenario plans for different risk scenarios, outlining steps to take if specific risks materialize. Scenario planning helps you respond swiftly and strategically.

Regulatory Compliance

Stay updated on regulatory changes that could impact your business. Develop a compliance strategy to ensure your operations adhere to relevant laws and regulations.

Strategic Partnerships

Cultivate strategic partnerships that can provide support in case of operational disruptions. Collaborative efforts can enhance your business's resilience.

Continuous Monitoring

Continuously monitor your business's financial and operational health. Regularly review key metrics and indicators to detect potential risks early.

Employee Training

Train your employees to be aware of risks and how to respond in case of emergencies. A knowledgeable and prepared team can mitigate operational risks.

Crisis Management Plan

Develop a comprehensive crisis management plan that outlines roles, responsibilities, communication strategies, and actions to take during a crisis.

Managing financial and operational risks is not just about defense; it's about building a foundation of resilience. As you immerse yourself in this chapter, remember that preparedness is your shield against uncertainties. Your mastery of this art empowers you to create a symphony of stability, foresight, and progress. Just as a fortress is fortified to withstand challenges, so too must you fortify your business, ensuring that it remains strong and steady even in the face of adversities, and that your business's journey toward growth and success continues uninterrupted.

Adapting to Changes in the Business Landscape

In the ever-changing landscape of business, adapting to shifts is the compass that guides your company's relevance and longevity. This chapter delves into the art of embracing change and navigating transitions – a strategic pursuit that involves staying attuned to market dynamics, fostering a culture of innovation, and making informed adjustments to align with evolving trends. Just as a skilled sailor adjusts the sails to harness changing winds, so too must you adjust your strategies to navigate the currents of change.

Market Monitoring and Analysis

Begin by consistently monitoring the business landscape for shifts in consumer behavior, technological advancements, competitive dynamics, and regulatory changes.

Agile Decision-Making

Foster a culture of agile decision-making within your organization. Encourage teams to adapt quickly to changing circumstances and make timely adjustments.

Innovation and Creativity

Empower your team to think innovatively and explore creative solutions. Innovation enables your business to stay ahead of the curve.

Customer-Centric Approach

Place your customers at the center of your strategies. Continuously seek feedback, understand their changing needs, and adapt your offerings accordingly.

Technology Integration

Embrace technological advancements that can enhance your business operations and customer experiences. Leverage digital tools to streamline processes and engagement.

Competitor Analysis

Regularly analyze your competitors' strategies and performance. Identify shifts in their approaches and assess their potential impact on your business.

Scenario Planning

Develop scenario plans for various potential changes in the business landscape. Preparing for different scenarios helps you respond strategically.

Adaptable Leadership

Lead with adaptability and openness to change. Be willing to pivot and adjust your strategies based on new information and market shifts.

Resource Allocation

Allocate resources strategically to support new initiatives or areas of focus that arise due to changes in the business environment.

Strategic Partnerships

Cultivate partnerships that can provide expertise or resources to navigate changes. Collaborations can amplify your capacity to adapt.

Learning Culture

Create a culture of continuous learning and improvement. Encourage employees to seek out new knowledge and skills that align with changing demands.

Effective Communication

Maintain open and transparent communication with your team and stakeholders. Sharing insights and decisions promotes alignment and understanding.

Adapting to changes in the business landscape is not just about survival; it's about thriving amid evolution. As you delve into this chapter, remember that change is a constant opportunity for growth. Your mastery of this art empowers you to create a symphony of flexibility, innovation, and progress. Just as a skilled sailor adjusts sails to navigate changing waters, so too must you adjust your strategies to navigate the currents of change, ensuring that your business's journey remains on course toward continued success and evolution.

Scaling Responsibly and Sustainably

In the ever-evolving landscape of business, scaling responsibly and sustainably is the guiding principle that ensures your company's growth is both impactful and enduring. This chapter delves into the art of expanding your business while prioritizing ethical considerations, minimizing environmental impact, and fostering long-term viability – a strategic pursuit that involves meticulous planning, conscious resource management, and a dedication to social and environmental responsibility. Just as a conductor orchestrates a harmonious symphony, so too must you orchestrate your business's growth with a balanced and sustainable approach.

Ethical Growth Assessment

Begin by evaluating the ethical implications of your growth strategies. Consider how your expansion might affect employees, customers, communities, and stakeholders.

Environmental Stewardship

Prioritize environmental sustainability by adopting practices that reduce your business's carbon footprint, conserve resources, and minimize waste.

Social Impact

Align your growth plans with positive social impact. Seek ways to contribute to communities, support social causes, and create a positive work environment.

Values-Driven Culture

Foster a values-driven culture that aligns with responsible growth. Ensure that employees, partners, and stakeholders share a commitment to sustainability.

Circular Economy

Adopt principles of the circular economy by designing products for durability, repairability, and recyclability to minimize waste and promote sustainability.

Transparency and Accountability

Communicate your commitment to responsible growth transparently. Be accountable for your actions and progress toward sustainability goals.

Inclusive Business Practices

Incorporate inclusivity into your growth strategies. Support diversity, equity, and inclusion both within your organization and in your engagement with stakeholders.

Strategic Partnerships

Forge partnerships with organizations that share your values and can contribute to responsible growth. Collaboration can amplify your impact.

Long-Term Planning

Plan for sustainable growth over the long term. Consider how your decisions today will shape the future of your business and its impact.

Measuring Impact

Implement metrics to quantify the social, environmental, and economic impact of your growth. Regularly assess your progress and adapt strategies accordingly.

Innovation for Sustainability

Promote innovation that addresses sustainability challenges. Develop products, services, and processes that contribute to a more sustainable future.

Ethical Leadership

Lead by example with a commitment to ethical leadership. Your actions and decisions set the tone for responsible growth throughout your organization.

Scaling responsibly and sustainably is not just about growth; it's about leaving a positive legacy for generations to come. As you immerse yourself in this chapter, remember that your business's impact extends beyond profit. Your mastery of this art empowers you to create a symphony of purpose, stewardship, and progress. Just as a conductor guides an orchestra to create a harmonious masterpiece, so too must you guide your business to scale responsibly and sustainably, ensuring that its journey resonates with ethical purpose and contributes to a more prosperous and sustainable future.

Balancing Growth with Sustainability

In the dynamic landscape of business, balancing growth with sustainability is the compass that ensures your company's expansion is both prosperous and environmentally responsible. This chapter delves into the art of achieving growth while minimizing ecological impact, fostering social responsibility, and maintaining long-term viability – a strategic pursuit that involves harmonizing economic success with environmental stewardship. Just as a skilled tightrope walker maintains equilibrium between two ends, so too must you navigate the delicate balance between growth and sustainability.

Holistic Growth Approach

Begin by adopting a holistic perspective that considers economic, environmental, and social aspects of growth. Recognize that sustainable practices contribute to long-term success.

Environmental Footprint Reduction

Prioritize strategies that reduce your business's environmental footprint. Implement energy-efficient technologies, reduce waste, and explore renewable resources.

Circular Business Model

Embrace circular economy principles by designing products for durability, repair, and recycling. Extend product lifecycles and minimize waste generation.

Sustainable Supply Chain

Optimize your supply chain for sustainability. Partner with suppliers who share your commitment to ethical practices and responsible sourcing.

Inclusive Business Practices

Foster inclusivity by promoting diversity and equity within your organization and engaging with diverse stakeholders. Inclusivity aligns with sustainability goals.

Ethical Consumerism

Cater to the growing demand for ethically produced and environmentally friendly products. Align your offerings with consumer preferences for sustainability.

Carbon Neutrality Goals

Set ambitious carbon neutrality goals and work toward reducing your business's carbon emissions. Invest in offset projects and renewable energy sources.

Transparency and Reporting

Communicate your sustainability efforts transparently. Publish regular reports detailing your progress toward environmental and social goals.

Social Impact Investment

Allocate resources to initiatives that have a positive impact on local communities. Support social projects and contribute to sustainable development.

Sustainable Innovation

Channel innovation toward sustainable solutions. Develop products and services that address environmental challenges and meet customer needs.

Leadership Commitment

Lead by example with a strong commitment to sustainability. Cultivate a culture that values responsible growth and integrates it into daily operations.

Balanced Decision-Making

Strive for balanced decision-making that accounts for economic, social, and environmental factors. Evaluate potential trade-offs and make informed choices.

Balancing growth with sustainability is not just about equilibrium; it's about shaping a brighter future for both your business and the world. As you delve into this chapter, remember that responsible growth is an investment in long-term prosperity. Your mastery of this art empowers you to create a symphony of progress, responsibility, and success. Just as a tightrope walker maintains poise to cross a challenging path, so too must you navigate the journey of growth and sustainability, ensuring that your business's trajectory remains steady, impactful, and in harmony with the world around it.

Ethical Considerations in Business Expansion

In the expansive journey of business, ethical considerations in expansion serve as the compass that guides your company's growth with integrity and accountability. This chapter delves into the art of expanding your business while upholding ethical principles, respecting stakeholders, and contributing positively to society – a strategic pursuit that involves conscious decision-making, transparency, and a commitment to doing what is right. Just as a navigator charts a course with moral compass in hand, so too must you steer your business's expansion with a clear sense of ethical direction.

Stakeholder Alignment

Begin by identifying and understanding the needs and expectations of various stakeholders, including employees, customers, investors, suppliers, and local communities.

Code of Ethics

Establish a comprehensive code of ethics that outlines the values and principles guiding your business's expansion. Communicate these standards to all stakeholders.

Social Impact Assessment

Conduct a thorough assessment of the potential social impact of your expansion. Consider how it might affect local communities, employees, and broader society.

Environmental Responsibility

Prioritize environmentally responsible practices in your expansion plans. Minimize negative ecological impacts and explore ways to contribute positively to the environment.

Fair Labor Practices

Ensure fair treatment of employees throughout the expansion process. Uphold labor standards, promote diversity, and provide growth opportunities.

Transparency and Accountability

Practice transparency in all aspects of your expansion. Communicate your plans, actions, and progress openly to stakeholders.

Responsible Marketing

Adopt ethical marketing practices that avoid misinformation, manipulation, and exploitation. Be honest and transparent in your communications with customers.

Community Engagement

Engage with local communities where you plan to expand. Listen to their concerns, seek input, and contribute positively to their well-being.

Supply Chain Ethics

Extend ethical considerations to your supply chain. Partner with suppliers who share your commitment to ethical and responsible practices.

Anti-Corruption Measures

Implement anti-corruption policies and practices to ensure that your expansion remains free from unethical influence or practices.

Philanthropy and Giving Back

Incorporate philanthropic efforts into your expansion plans. Contribute to charitable initiatives that align with your business's values and social impact goals.

Long-Term Sustainability

Consider the long-term sustainability of your expansion. Will your growth be compatible with the well-being of future generations?

Ethical considerations in business expansion are not just about growth; they're about making a positive impact on the world. As you immerse yourself in this chapter, remember that ethical expansion is a testament to your commitment to doing good. Your mastery of this art empowers you to create a symphony of integrity, responsibility, and progress. Just as a navigator charts a course that respects both the destination and the journey, so too must you steer your business's expansion in a manner that honors ethical values and ensures a legacy of positive influence and success.

Long-Term Planning for Continued Success

In the far-reaching landscape of business, long-term planning is the compass that ensures your company's journey remains on a path of sustained success. This chapter delves into the art of strategic foresight, encompassing visionary thinking, adaptable strategies, and a commitment to evolving with the times – a pursuit that involves aligning short-term actions with long-term goals. Just as a skilled architect envisions a building's grandeur before laying the foundation, so too must you envision your business's future and lay the groundwork for enduring prosperity.

Visionary Thinking

Begin by envisioning where you want your business to be in the distant future. Set ambitious goals that inspire and drive your long-term planning.

SWOT Analysis for the Long-Term

Conduct a SWOT analysis with a focus on long-term considerations. Evaluate strengths, weaknesses, opportunities, and threats that might impact your business's sustainability.

Future Trends and Industry Shifts

Stay attuned to emerging trends and shifts within your industry. Anticipate changes that might impact your business and adapt your strategies accordingly.

Strategic Roadmap

Develop a strategic roadmap that outlines the steps needed to achieve your long-term goals. Break down milestones and initiatives to ensure steady progress.

Adaptive Strategies

Craft adaptable strategies that can flexibly respond to changing circumstances. Build in contingencies to adjust your course as needed.

Innovation and Research

Invest in research and innovation to stay ahead of the curve. Develop new products, services, and processes that can position your business for long-term success.

Talent Development

Cultivate a pipeline of skilled employees and leaders who can drive your business's success in the long term. Invest in their training and development.

Customer-Centric Approach

Prioritize a customer-centric approach that builds strong relationships and fosters loyalty over the long haul. Satisfied customers are more likely to stay with your brand.

Financial Resilience

Maintain a solid financial foundation to weather economic fluctuations and challenges. Build reserves and manage debt responsibly.

Technology Integration

Leverage technology to enhance efficiency, innovation, and scalability. Stay updated on tech trends that can bolster your business's long-term competitiveness.

Sustainability and Responsibility

Integrate ethical and sustainable practices into your long-term planning. Consider your business's impact on the environment and society as you grow.

Legacy Planning

Think beyond your tenure as a leader. Consider the legacy you want to leave for the next generation of your business and plan accordingly.

Long-term planning for continued success is not just about setting goals; it's about shaping a legacy. As you delve into this chapter, remember that the journey of success is an ongoing endeavor. Your mastery of this art empowers you to create a symphony of foresight, adaptability, and progress. Just as an architect envisions a building's grandeur before it stands tall, so too must you envision your business's future, building its foundation with strategic intent and navigating the path to enduring success.

Conclusion

As you reach the final notes of this journey through the intricacies of business growth, envision the symphony you have composed — a symphony of strategy, innovation, resilience, and ethics. Just as a composer carefully crafts each note to create a harmonious masterpiece, so too have you crafted a path toward the symphony of success for your business.

You've learned to conduct the intricate melody of understanding your market, identifying opportunities, and adapting to change. You've composed harmonies of branding, marketing, and customer engagement, resonating with your audience. You've orchestrated the rhythm of responsible growth, balancing financial goals with ethical considerations and sustainable practices.

Throughout this exploration, you've become a conductor of strategies, leading your business through challenges and opportunities, navigating storms and calm waters alike. You've embraced a mindset of innovation, adaptation, and continuous improvement, ensuring that your business remains relevant in an ever-changing world.

Your symphony is not just a collection of chapters; it's a testament to your dedication, creativity, and determination. It's the blueprint for achieving growth and success while maintaining integrity and responsibility. As you apply the insights gathered here, remember that every decision you make shapes your business's melody, contributing to a harmonious legacy that resonates far into the future.

So, take these lessons, insights, and strategies, and compose the symphony of your business's success. Lead with purpose, innovation, and a commitment to making a positive impact. Just as a conductor brings an orchestra to its crescendo, so too can you lead your business to its pinnacle of achievement, creating a masterpiece that leaves a lasting impression on your industry, your community, and the world.

Celebrating Milestones and Achievements

In the grand performance of business, celebrating milestones and achievements is the ovation that acknowledges your company's progress, honors your team's dedication, and marks the rhythm of success. This chapter delves into the art of recognizing and commemorating significant moments – a strategic pursuit that involves fostering a culture of appreciation, reinforcing motivation, and acknowledging the collective efforts that have propelled your business forward. Just as a standing ovation salutes a memorable performance, so too must you celebrate the moments that define your business's journey.

Importance of Celebration

Begin by understanding the significance of celebrating milestones. Recognition and celebration create a sense of accomplishment and boost morale.

Acknowledging Team Efforts

Recognize that achievements are the results of collective efforts. Celebrate the contributions of every team member who played a role in reaching a milestone.

Setting Meaningful Milestones

Establish meaningful milestones that align with your business's goals and values. Milestones should mark progress and motivate continued growth.

Cultivating a Culture of Appreciation

Foster a culture of appreciation where recognizing achievements becomes a routine practice. Acknowledge small wins and major accomplishments alike.

Customized Recognition

Tailor recognition to suit individual preferences. Some team members might appreciate public acknowledgment, while others prefer private recognition.

Public Celebration

Hold public celebrations to highlight major achievements. Share success stories with your team, stakeholders, and even the broader community.

Personalized Rewards

Consider offering personalized rewards that reflect the interests and aspirations of team members who contributed to a milestone.

Learning and Reflection

Use milestones as opportunities for learning and reflection. Analyze the journey, gather feedback, and identify areas for improvement.

Long-Term Vision

Connect milestones to your long-term vision. Show how each achievement contributes to the larger narrative of your business's success.

Camaraderie and Team Bonding

Use celebrations to foster camaraderie and strengthen team bonds. Shared celebrations create a sense of unity and belonging.

Inspiring Future Success

Celebrate not only past achievements but also the potential for future success. Use celebrations to ignite motivation for the next stages of growth.

Celebrating milestones and achievements is not just about applause; it's about recognizing the collective symphony of dedication, innovation, and effort. As you reflect on this chapter, remember that celebration amplifies success and strengthens the ties that bind your team together. Your mastery of this art empowers you to create a symphony of gratitude, motivation, and progress. Just as an encore extends the applause for an outstanding performance, so too must you extend your appreciation for the continuous symphony of achievements that shape your business's journey toward greatness.

Looking Ahead: The Journey of Continuous Growth

As you stand at the crossroads of accomplishment and aspiration, the journey of continuous growth beckons with new horizons and untapped potential. This final chapter encapsulates the essence of the road ahead – a road paved with opportunities, challenges, and uncharted territories. It's a journey that embraces the symphony of evolution, innovation, and progress, a journey that reminds you that growth is not a destination, but a perpetual melody that propels your business forward.

Embracing Change

Prepare to embrace change as an integral part of the journey. Change brings fresh perspectives, new ideas, and the chance to pivot toward new avenues of growth.

Cultivating Adaptability

Cultivate a mindset of adaptability. A willingness to adjust, evolve, and learn from experience will guide you through the twists and turns of the path ahead.

Innovating and Iterating

Prioritize innovation as a cornerstone of your journey. Continuously explore new technologies, trends, and strategies to stay ahead in the ever-evolving business landscape.

Global Perspective

Expand your horizons by considering global opportunities. The interconnected world presents chances to tap into new markets and diverse customer bases.

Mindful Scaling

Scale your business responsibly, considering both growth and sustainability. Each step forward should be aligned with your values and long-term vision.

Nurturing Relationships

Foster relationships with customers, partners, and stakeholders. These connections provide the foundation for collaboration and mutual growth.

Learning and Resilience

Approach challenges as opportunities for learning and growth. Resilience in the face of setbacks is a key attribute of businesses that thrive over time.

Strategic Exploration

Continue to explore new avenues and niches that align with your expertise. Diversification can open doors to previously unimagined possibilities.

Legacy of Impact

Keep in mind the legacy you want to leave through your business. Make decisions that contribute positively to the world and inspire future generations.

Celebrating Progress

Celebrate not only major milestones but also the smaller victories along the way. These celebrations fuel motivation and create a positive atmosphere.

Evolving Leadership

Adapt your leadership style to the changing needs of your business. A leader who evolves can inspire and guide their team to greater heights.

As you embark on the journey of continuous growth, remember that you are the conductor of your business's symphony. With each decision, innovation, and adaptation, you shape the melody that echoes through time. Your mastery of this art empowers you to navigate the ever-changing currents, creating a symphony that resonates with progress, leadership, and impact. Just as a composer composes a symphony with countless notes, so too must you compose the symphony of your business's journey, orchestrating a harmonious narrative of growth, innovation, and a legacy that reverberates long into the future.